BAR-ROOM BALLADS

A Book of Verse

By

ROBERT SERVICE

Author of "Songs of a Sourdough"
"Rhymes of a Red Cross Man", etc.

London
ERNEST BENN LIMITED

First Published May 1940
Second Impression April 1942

Printed in Great Britain by the KEMP HALL PRESS LTD.
in the City of Oxford

CONTENTS

6 CONTENTS

Fore=warning

I'd rather be the Jester than the Minstrel of the King;
I'd rather jangle cap and bells than twang the stately
    harp;
I'd rather make His royal ribs with belly-laughter ring,
Than see him sitting in the suds and sulky as a carp.
I'd rather be the Court buffoon than its most high=
   browed sage:
        So you who read, take heed, take heed—
        Ere yet you turn my page.

PRELUDE

To smite Apollo's lyre I am unable ;
Of loveliness, alas! I cannot sing.
My lot it is, across the tavern table,
To start a chorus to the strumming string.
I have no gift to touch your heart to pity ;
I have no power to ring the note of pain :
All I can do is pipe a pothouse ditty,
Or roar a Rabelaisian refrain.

Behold yon minstrel of the empty belly,
Who seeks to please the bored and waiting throng,
Outside the Opera with ukelele,
And raucous strains of syncopated song.
His rag-time mocks their eager hearts a-hunger
For golden voices, melody divine :
Yet . . . throw a penny to the ballad-monger ;
Yet . . . listen idly to this song of mine.

For with a humble heart I clank rhyme's fetters,
And bare my buttocks to the critic knout ;
A graceless hobo in the Land of Letters,

Piping my ditties of the down-and-out.
A bar-room bard ... so if a coin you're flinging,
Pay me a pot, and let me dream and boose ;
To stars of scorn my dour defiance ringing,
With battered banjo and a strumpet Muse.

THE BALLAD OF SALVATION BILL

'TWAS in the bleary middle of the hard-boiled
    Arctic night,
I was lonesome as a loon, so if you can,
Imagine my emotions of amazement and delight
When I bumped into that Missionary Man.
He was lying lost and dying in the moon's unholy
    leer,
And frozen from his toes to finger-tips ;
The famished wolf-pack ringed him ; but he
    didn't seem to fear,
As he pressed his ice-bound Bible to his lips.

'Twas the limit of my trap-line, with the cabin
    miles away,
And every step was like a stab of pain ;
But I packed him like a baby, and I nursed him
    night and day,
Till I got him back to health and strength again.

So there we were, benighted in the shadow of the
　　Pole,
And he might have proved a priceless little pard,
If he hadn't got to worrying about my blessed
　　soul,
And a-quotin' me his Bible by the yard.

Now there was I, a husky guy, whose god was
　　Nicotine,
With a " coffin-nail " a fixture in my mug ;
I rolled them in the pages of a pulpwood magazine,
And hacked them with my jack-knife from the
　　plug.
For, Oh to know the bliss and glow that good
　　tobacco means,
Just live among the everlasting ice. . . .
So judge my horror when I found my stock of
　　magazines
Was chewed into a chowder by the mice.

A woeful week went by and not a single pill I
　　had,
Me that would smoke my forty in a day ;

I sighed, I swore, I strode the floor ; I felt I
    would go mad :
The gospel-plugger watched me in dismay.
My brow was wet, my teeth were set, my nerves
    were rasping raw ;
And yet that preacher couldn't understand :
So with despair I wrestled there—when suddenly
    I saw
The volume he was holding in his hand.

Then something snapped inside my brain, and
    with an evil start
The wolf-man in me woke to rabid rage.
" I saved your lousy life," says I ; " so show you
    have a heart,
And tear me out a solitary page."
He shrank and shrivelled at my words ; his face
    went pewter white ;
'Twas just as if I'd handed him a blow ;
And then . . . and then he seemed to swell, and
    grow to Heaven's height,
And in a voice that rang he answered : " No! "

I grabbed my loaded rifle and I jabbed it to his
    chest :

"Come on, you shrimp, give up that Book," says
    I.
Well sir, he was a parson, but he stacked up with
    the best,
And for grit I got to hand it to the guy.
"If I should let you desecrate this Holy Word,"
    he said,
"My soul would be eternally accurst ;
So go on, Bill, I'm ready. You can pump me
    full of lead
And take it, but—you've got to kill me first."

Now I'm no foul assassin, though I'm full of sin-
    ful ways,
And I knew right there the fellow had me beat ;
For I felt a yellow mongrel in the glory of his
    gaze,
And I flung my foolish firearm at his feet.
Then wearily I turned away, and dropped upon
    my bunk,
And there I lay and blubbered like a kid.
"Forgive me, pard," says I at last, "for acting
    like a skunk,
But hide the blasted rifle. . . ." Which he did.

And he also hid his Bible, which was maybe just
    as well,
For the sight of all that paper gave me pain ;
And there were crimson moments when I felt I'd
    go to hell
To have a single cigarette again.
And so I lay day after day, and brooded dark and
    deep,
Until one night I thought I'd end it all ;
Then rough I roused the preacher, where he
    stretched pretending sleep,
With his map of horror turned towards the wall.

" See here, my pious pal," says I, " I've stood it
    long enough. . . .
Behold ! I've mixed some strychnine in a cup ;
Enough to kill a dozen men—believe me it's no
    bluff ;
Now watch me, for I'm gonna drink it up.
You've seen me bludgeoned by despair through
    bitter days and nights,
And now you'll see me squirming as I die.
You're not to blame, you've played the game
    according to your lights. . . .

But how would Christ have played it ?—Well,
　　good-bye. . . ."

With that I raised the deadly drink and laid it to
　　my lips,
But he was on me with a tiger-bound ;
And as we locked and reeled and rocked with
　　wild and wicked grips,
The poison cup went crashing to the ground.
" Don't do it, Bill," he madly shrieked. " May-
　　be I acted wrong.
See, here's my Bible—use it as you will ;
But promise me—you'll read a little as you go
　　along. . . .
You do ! Then take it, Brother ; smoke your fill."

And so I did. I smoked and smoked from
　　Genesis to Job,
And as I smoked I read each blessed word ;
While in the shadow of his bunk I heard him sigh
　　and sob,
And then . . . a most peculiar thing occurred.
I got to reading more and more, and smoking less
　　and less,

Till just about the day his heart was broke,
Says I: " Here, take it back, me lad. I've had
    enough, I guess.
Your paper makes a mighty rotten smoke."

So then and there with plea and prayer he
    wrestled for my soul,
And I was racked and ravaged by regrets.
But God was good, for lo! next day there came
    the police patrol,
With paper for a thousand cigarettes. . . .
So now I'm called Salvation Bill; I teach the
    Living Law,
And bally-hoo the Bible with the best ;
And if a guy won't listen—why, I sock him on
    the jaw,
And preach the Gospel sitting on his chest.

B

EACH DAY A LIFE

I COUNT each day a little life,
　　With birth and death complete ;
I cloister it from care and strife
　　And keep it sane and sweet.

With eager eyes I greet the morn,
　　Exultant as a boy,
Knowing that I am newly born
　　To wonder and to joy.

And when the sunset splendours wane,
　　And ripe for rest am I,
Knowing that I will live again,
　　Exultantly I die.

O that all Life were but a Day
　　Sunny and sweet and sane !
And that at Even I might say :
　　" I sleep to wake again."

DOLLS

SHE said : " I am too old to play
With dolls," and put them all away,
Into a box, one rainy day.

I think she must have felt some pain,
She looked so long into the rain,
Then sighed : " I'll bring you out again ;

" For I'll have little children too,
With sunny hair and eyes of blue,
And they will play and play with you.

" And now good-bye, my pretty dears ;
There in the dark for years and years,
Dream of your little mother's tears."

Eglantine, Pierrot and Marie Claire,
Topsy and Tiny and Teddy Bear,
Side by side in the coffer there.

Time went by ; one day she kneeled
By a wooden Cross in Flanders Field,
And wept for the One the earth concealed ;

And made a vow she would never wed,
But always be true to the deathless dead,
Until the span of her life be sped.

     .   .   .   .   .

More years went on and they made her wise
By sickness and pain and sacrifice,
With greying tresses and tired eyes.

And then one evening of weary rain,
She opened the old oak box again,
And her heart was clutched with an ancient pain.

For there in the quiet dark they lay,
Just as they were when she put them away . . .
O but it seemed like yesterday !

Topsy and Tiny and Teddy Bear,
Eglantine, Pierrot and Marie Claire,
Ever so hopefully waiting there.

But she looked at them through her blinding
    tears,

And she said : " You've been patient, my pretty
    dears ;
You've waited and waited all these years.

" I've broken a promise I made so true ;
But my heart, my darlings, is broken too :
No little Mothers have I for you.

" My hands are withered, my hair is grey ;
Yet just for a moment I'll try to play
With you as I did that long dead day. . . .

" Ah no, I cannot. I try in vain. . . .
I stare and I stare into the rain. . . .
I'll put you back in your box again.

" Bless you, darlings, perhaps one day,
Some little Mother will find you and play,
And once again you'll be glad and gay.

" But when in the friendly dark I lie,
No one will ever love you as I. . . .
My little children . . . good-bye . . . good-bye."

THE BALLAD OF HOW MACPHERSON HELD THE FLOOR

Said President MacConnachie to Treasurer Mac-
Call :

" We ought to have a piper for our next Saint
Andrew's Ball.

Yon squakin' saxophone gives me the syncopated
gripes.

I'm sick of jazz, I want to hear the skirling of the
pipes."

" Alas ! it's true," said Tam MacCall.   " The
young folk of to-day

Are fox-trot mad and dinna ken a reel from a
Strathspey.

Now, what we want's a kiltie lad, primed up wi'
mountain dew,

To strut the floor at supper time, and play a lilt or
two.

In all the North there's only one ; of him I've
heard them speak :

His name is Jock MacPherson, and he lives on
    Boulder Creek ;
An old-time hard-rock miner, and a wild and
    wastrel loon,
Who spends his nights in glory, playing pibrochs
    to the moon.
I'll seek him out ; beyond a doubt on next Saint
    Andrew's night
We'll proudly hear the pipes to cheer and charm
    our appetite."

Oh lads were neat and lassies sweet who graced
    Saint Andrew's Ball ;
But there was none so full of fun as Treasurer
    MacCall.
And as Maloney's rag-time band struck up the
    newest hit,
He smiled a smile behind his hand, and chuckled :
    " Wait a bit."
And so with many a Celtic snort, with malice in
    his eye,
He watched the merry crowd cavort, till supper
    time drew nigh.
Then gleefully he seemed to steal, and sought the
    Nugget Bar,

Wherein there sat a tartaned chiel, as lonely as a
    star ;
A huge and hairy Highlandman as hearty as a
    breeze,
A glass of whisky in his hand, his bag-pipes on
    his knees.
" Drink down your *doch and doris*, Jock," cried
    Treasurer MacCall ;
" The time is ripe to up and pipe ; they wait you
    in the hall.
Gird up your loins and grit your teeth, and here's
    a pint of hooch
To mind you of your native heath—jist pit it in
    your pooch.
Play on and on for all you're worth ; you'll shame
    us if you stop.
Remember you're of Scottish birth—keep piping
    till you drop.
Aye, though a bunch of Willie boys should bluster
    and implore,
For the glory of the Highlands, lad, you've *got* to
    hold the floor."

The dancers were at supper, and the tables
    groaned with cheer,

When President MacConnachie exclaimed :
    " What do I hear ?
Methinks it's like a chanter, and it's coming
    from the hall."
" It's Jock MacPherson tuning up," cried
    Treasurer MacCall.
So up they jumped with shouts of glee, and gaily
    hurried forth.
Said they : " We never thought to see a piper in
    the North."
Aye, all the lads and lassies braw went buzzing
    out like bees,
And Jock MacPherson there they saw, with red
    and rugged knees.
Full six feet four he strode the floor, a grizzled
    son of Skye,
With glory in his whiskers and with whisky in
    his eye.
With skelping stride and Scottish pride he
    towered above them all :
" And is he no' a bonny sight ? " said Treasurer
    MacCall.
While President MacConnachie was fairly daft
    with glee,

And there was jubilation in the Scottish Commy-
tee.

But the dancers seemed uncertain, and they
signified their doubt,

By dashing back to eat as fast as they had darted
out.

And someone raised the question 'twixt the coffee
and the cakes :

" Does the Piper walk to get away from all the
noise he makes ? "

Then reinforced with fancy food they slowly
trickled forth,

And watched in patronizing mood the Piper of
the North.

Proud, proud was Jock MacPherson, as he made
his bag-pipes skirl,

And he set his sporran swinging, and he gave his
kilts a whirl.

And President MacConnachie was jumping like
a flea,

And there was joy and rapture in the Scottish
Commy-tee.

" Jist let them have their saxophones, wi' con-
stipated squall ;

We're having heaven's music now," said Treasurer MacCall.

But the dancers waxed impatient, and they rather
seemed to fret

For Maloney and the jazz of his Hibernian
Quartette.

Yet little recked the Piper, as he swung with head
on high,

Lamenting with MacCrimmon on the heather
hills of Skye.

With Highland passion in his heart he held the
centre floor ;

Aye, Jock MacPherson played as he had never
played before.

Maloney's Irish melodists were sitting in their
place,

And as Maloney waited, there was wonder in his
face.

'Twas sure the gorgeous music—Golly ! wouldn't
it be grand

If he could get MacPherson as a member of his
band ?

But the dancers moped and mumbled, as around
the room they sat :

" We paid to dance," they grumbled ; " But we
　　cannot dance to *that*.

Of course we're not denying that it's really
　　splendid stuff ;

But it's mighty satisfying—don't you think we've
　　had enough ? "

" You've raised a pretty problem," answered
　　Treasurer MacCall ;

" For on Saint Andrew's Night, ye ken, the Piper
　　rules the Ball."

Said President MacConnachie : " You've said a
　　solemn thing.

Tradition holds him sacred, and he's got to have
　　his fling.

But soon, no doubt, he'll weary out.　Have
　　patience ;　bide a wee."

" That's right.　Respect the Piper," said the
　　Scottish Commy-tee.

And so MacPherson stalked the floor, and fast the
　　moments flew,

Till half an hour went past, as irritation grew and
　　grew.

Then the dancers held a council, and with faces
　　fiercely set,

They hailed Maloney, heading his Hibernian
    Quartette :
" It's long enough we've waited. Come on,
    Mike, play up the Blues."
And Maloney hesitated, but he didn't dare refuse.
So banjo and piano, and guitar and saxophone
Contended with the shrilling of the chanter and
    the drone ;
And the women's ears were muffled, so infernal
    was the din,
But MacPherson was unruffled, for he knew that
    he would win.
Then two bright boys jazzed round him, and
    they sought to play the clown,
But MacPherson jolted sideways, and the Sasse-
    nachs went down.
And as if it was a signal, with a wild and angry
    roar,
The gates of wrath were riven—yet MacPherson
    held the floor.

Aye, amid the rising tumult, still he strode with
    head on high,
With ribbands gaily streaming, yet with battle in
    his eye.

Amid the storm that gathered, still he stalked
    with Highland pride,
While President and Treasurer sprang bravely to
    his side.
And with ire and indignation that was glorious to
    see,
Around him in a body ringed the Scottish
    Commy-tee.
Their teeth were clenched with fury ; their eyes
    with anger blazed :
" Ye manna touch the Piper," was the slogan that
    they raised.
Then blows were struck, and men went down ;
    yet 'mid the rising fray
MacPherson towered in triumph—and he never
    ceased to play.

Alas! his faithful followers were but a gallant few,
And faced defeat, although they fought with all
    the skill they knew.
For President MacConnachie was seen to slip
    and fall,
And o'er his prostrate body stumbled Treasurer
    MacCall.

And as their foes with triumph roared, and
    leaguered them about,
It looked as if their little band would soon be
    counted out.
For eyes were black and noses red, yet on that
    field of gore,
As resolute as Highland rock—MacPherson held
    the floor.

Maloney watched the battle, and his brows were
    bleakly set,
While with him paused and panted his Hibernian
    Quartette.
For sure it is an evil spite, and breaking to the
    heart,
For Irishmen to watch a fight and not be taking
    part.
Then suddenly on high he soared, and tightened
    up his belt :
" And shall we see them crush," he roared, " a
    brother and a Celt ?
A fellow *artiste* needs our aid. Come on, boys,
    take a hand."
Then down into the *mêlée* dashed Maloney and
    his band.

Now though it was Saint Andrew's Ball, yet men
    of every race,
That bow before the Great God Jazz were
    gathered in that place.
Yea, there were those who grunt : " Ya! Ya! "
    and those who squeak : " We! We! "
Likewise Dutch, Dago, Swede and Finn, Polak
    and Portugee.
Yet like ripe grain before the gale that national
    hotch-potch
Went down before the fury of the Irish and the
    Scotch.
Aye, though they closed their gaping ranks and
    rallied to the fray,
To the Shamrock and the Thistle went the glory
    of the day.

You should have seen the carnage in the drooling
    light of dawn,
Yet 'mid the scene of slaughter Jock MacPherson
    playing on.
Though all lay low about him, yet he held his
    head on high,
And piped as if he stood upon the caller crags of
    Skye.

His face was grim as granite, and no favour did
    he ask,
Though weary were his mighty lungs and empty
    was his flask.
And when a fallen foe wailed out : " Say! when
    will you have done ? "
MacPherson grinned and answered : " Hoots !
    She'll only haf' begun."
Aye, though his hands were bloody, and his
    knees were gay with gore, .
A Grampian of Highland pride—MacPherson
    held the floor.

And still in Yukon valleys where the silent peaks
    look down,
They tell of how the Piper was invited up to
    town,
And he went in kilted glory, and he piped before
    them all,
But he wouldn't stop his piping till he busted up
    the Ball.
Of that Homeric scrap they speak, and how the
    fight went on,
With sally and with rally till the breaking of the
    dawn.

C

And how the Piper towered like a rock amid the
    fray,
And the battle surged about him, but he never
    ceased to play.
Aye, by the lonely camp-fires, still they tell the
    story o'er—
How the Sassenach was vanquished and—Mac-
    Pherson held the floor.

GIPSY

THE poppies that in Spring I sow,
In rings of radiance gleam and glow,
Like lords and ladies gay.
A joy are they to dream beside,
As in the air of eventide
They flutter, dip and sway.

For some are scarlet, some are gold,
While some in fairy flame unfold,
And some are rose and white.
There's pride of breeding in their glance,
And pride of beauty as they dance
Cotillions of delight.

Yet as I lift my eyes I see
Their swarthy kindred, wild and free,
Who flaunt it in the field.
" Begone, you Romanies ! " I say,
" Lest you defile this bright array
Whose loveliness I shield."

My poppies are a sheen of light ;
They take with ecstasy the sight,
And hold the heart elate. . . .
Yet why do I so often turn
To where their outcast brothers burn
With passion at my gate ?

My poppies are my joy and pride ;
Yet wistfully I gaze outside
To where their sisters yearn ;
Their blousy crimson cups afire,
Their lips aflutter with desire
To give without return.

My poppies dance a minuet;
Like courtiers in silk they set
My garden all aglow. . . .
Yet O the vagrants at my gate !
The gipsy trulls who peer and wait ! . . .
Calling the heart they know.

THE BALLAD OF HANK THE FINN

Now Fireman Flynn met Hank the Finn where
    lights of Lust-land glow ;
" Let's leave," says he, " the lousy sea, and give
    the land a show.
I'm fed up to the molar mark with wallopin' the
    brine ;
I feel the bloody barnacles a-carkin' on me spine.
Let's hit the hard-boiled North a crack, where
    creeks are paved with gold."
" You count me in," says Hank the Finn. " Ay
    do as Ay ban told."

And so they sought the Lonely Land and
    drifted down its stream,
Where sunny silence round them spanned, as
    dopey as a dream.
But to the spell of flood and fell their gold-grimed
    eyes were blind ;
By pine and peak they paused to seek, but no-
    thing did they find ;

No yellow glint of dust to mint, just mud and
    mocking sand,
And a hateful hush that seemed to crush them
    down on every hand.
Till Fireman Flynn grew mean as sin, and cursed
    his comrade cold,
But Hank the Finn would only grin, and . . . do
    as he was told.

Now Fireman Flynn had pieces ten of yellow
    Yankee gold,
Which every night he would invite his partner to
    behold.
" Look hard," says he ; " It's all you'll see in
    this god-blasted land ;
But don't you fret, I'm gonna let you hold them
    in your hand.
Yeah ! Watch 'em gleam then go and *dream*
    they're yours to have and hold."
Then Hank the Finn would scratch his chin and
    . . . do as he was told.

But every night by camp-fire light, he'd incubate
    his woes,

And fan the hate of mate for mate, the evil Arctic knows.

In dreams the Lapland witches gloomed like gargoyles overhead,

While the devils three of Helsinskee came cowering by his bed.

" Go, take," said they, " the yellow loot he's clinking in his belt,

And leave the sneaking wolverines to snout around his pelt.

Last night he called you *Swedish* scum, from out the glory-hole ;

To-day he said you were a bum, and damned your mother's soul.

Go, plug with lead his scurvy head, and grab his greasy gold. . . ."

Then Hank the Finn saw red within, and . . . did as he was told.

So in due course the famous Force of Men Who Get Their Man,

Swooped down on sleeping Hank the Finn, and popped him in the can.

And in due time his grievous crime was judged without a plea,

And he was dated up to swing upon the gallows
    tree.
Then Sheriff gave a party in the Law's almighty
    name,
He gave a neck-tie party, and he asked me to the
    same.
There was no hooch a-flowin' and his party
    wasn't gay,
For O our hearts were heavy at the dawning of
    the day.
There was no band a-playin' and the only dancin'
    there
Was Hank the Finn interpretin' his solo on the
    air.

We climbed the scaffold steps and stood beside
    the knotted rope.
We watched the hooded hangman and his eyes
    were dazed with dope.
The sheriff was in evening dress ; a bell began to
    toll,
A beastly bell that struck a knell of horror to the
    soul.
As if the doomed one was myself, I shuddered,
    waiting there.

I spoke no word, then . . . then I heard *his* step
    upon the stair ;
His halting foot, moccasin clad . . . and then I
    saw him stand
Between a weeping warder and a priest with
    Cross in hand.
And at the sight a murmur rose of terror and of
    awe,
And all them hardened gallows fans were sick at
    what they saw :
For as he towered above the mob, his limbs with
    leather triced,
By all that's wonderful, I swear, *his face was that
    of Christ.*

Now I ain't no blaspheming cuss, so don't you
    start to shout.
You see, his beard had grown so long it framed
    his face about.
His rippling hair was long and fair, his cheeks
    were spirit-pale,
His face was bright with holy light that made us
    wince and quail.
He looked at us with eyes a-shine, and sore were
    we confused,

As if he were the Judge divine, and we were the
    accused.
Aye, as serene he stood between the hangman
    and the cord,
You would have sworn, with anguish torn, he
    was the Blessed Lord.

The priest was wet with icy sweat, the Sheriff's
    lips were dry,
And we were staring starkly at the man who had
    to die.
" Lo! I am raised above you all," his pale lips
    seemed to say,
" For in a moment I shall leap to God's Eternal
    Day.
Am I not happy ! I forgive you each for what you
    do ;
Redeemed and penitent I go, with heart of love
    for you."

So there he stood in mystic mood, with scorn
    sublime of death.
I saw him gently kiss the Cross, and then I held
    my breath.

That blessed smile was blotted out ; they
    dropped the hood of black ;
They fixed the noose around his neck, the rope
    was hanging slack.
I heard him pray, I saw him sway, then . . . then
    he was not there ;
A rope, a ghastly yellow rope was jerking in the
    air ;
A jigging rope that soon was still ; a hush as of
    the tomb,
And Hank the Finn, that man of sin, had met his
    rightful doom.

His rightful doom ! Now that's the point. I'm
    wondering, because
I hold *a man is what he is,* and never what he
    was.
You see, the priest had filled that guy so full of
    holy dope,
That at the last he came to die as pious as the
    Pope.
A gentle ray of sunshine made a halo round his
    head.
I thought to see a sinner—lo ! I saw a Saint
    instead.

Aye, as he stood as martyrs stand, clean-cleansed
    of mortal dross,
I think he might have gloried had . . . WE NAILED
    HIM TO A CROSS.

SHIELA

When I played my penny whistle on the braes
    above Lochgyle
The heather bloomed about us, and we heard the
    peewit call ;
As you bent above your knitting something *fey*
    was in your smile,
And fine and soft and slow the rain made silver
    on your shawl.
Your cheeks were pink like painted cheeks, your
    eyes a pansy blue . . .
My heart was in my playing, but my music was
    for you.

And now I play the organ in this lordly London
    town ;
I play the lovely organ with a thousand folk in
    view.
They're wearing silk and satin, but I see a woollen
    gown,

And my heart's not in my music, for I'm thinking,
    lass, of you ;
When you listened to a barefoot boy, who piped
    of ancient pain,
And your ragged shawl was pearly in the sweet,
    shy rain.

I'll play them mighty music—O I'll make them
    stamp and cheer ;
I'll give the best that's in me, but I'll give it all
    for you.
I'll put my whole heart in it, for I feel that you
    are near,
Not yonder, sleeping always, where the peat is
    white with dew.
But I'll never live the rapture of that shepherd
    boy the while
I trilled for you my whistle on the braes above
    Lochgyle.

THE BALLAD OF TOUCH-THE-BUTTON NELL

Beyond the Rocking Bridge it lies, the burg of evil
    fame,
The huts where hive and swarm and thrive the
    sisterhood of shame.
Through all the night each cabin light goes out
    and then goes in,
A blood-red heliograph of lust, a semaphore of sin.
From Dawson Town, soft skulking down, each
    lewdster seeks his mate ;
And glad and bad, kimono clad, the wanton
    women wait.
The Klondike gossips to the moon, and simmers
    o'er its bars ;
Each silent hill is dark and chill, and chill the
    patient stars.
Yet hark ! upon the Rocking Bridge a baccanalian
    step ;

*A whispered : " Come," the skirl of some hell-
    raking demirep. . . .*

.   .   .   .   .   .

They gave a dance in Lousetown, and the Ten-
    derloin was there,
The girls were fresh and frolicsome, and nearly
    all were fair.
They flaunted on their backs the spoil of half-a-
    dozen towns ;
And some they blazed in gems of price, and some
    wore Paris gowns.
The voting was divided as to who might be the
    belle ;
But all opined, the winsomest was Touch-the-
    Button Nell.

Among the merry mob of men was one who did
    not dance,
But watched the " light fantastic " with a sour
    and sullen glance.
They saw his white teeth grit and gleam, they
    saw his thick lips twitch ;
They knew him for the giant Slav, one Riley
    Dooleyvitch.

" Oh Riley Dooleyvitch, come forth," quoth
    Touch-the-Button Nell,
" And dance a step or two with me—the music's
    simply swell."
He crushed her in his mighty arms, a meek,
    beguiling witch :
" With you, Oh Nell, I'd dance to Hell," said
    Riley Dooleyvitch.

He waltzed her up, he waltzed her down, he
    waltzed her round the hall ;
His heart was putty in her hands, his very soul
    was thrall.
As Antony of old succumbed to Cleopatra's spell,
So Riley Dooleyvitch bowed down to Touch-
    the-Button Nell.

" And do you love me true ? " she cried. " I love
    you as my life."
" How can you prove your love ? " she sighed.
    " I beg you, be my wife.
I stake big pay up Hunker way ; some day I be
    so rich ;
I make you shine in satins fine," said Riley
    Dooleyvitch.

D

" Some day you'll be so rich," she mocked ;
　　" That old pipe-dream don't go.
Who gets an option on this kid must have the
　　coin to show.
You work your ground. When Spring comes
　　round, our wedding bells will ring.
I'm on the square, and *I'll* take care of all the
　　gold you bring."

So Riley Dooleyvitch went back and worked
　　upon his claim ;
He ditched and drifted, sunk and stoped, with
　　one unswerving aim ;
And when his poke of raw moose-hide with dust
　　began to swell,
He brought and laid it at the feet of Touch-the-
　　Button Nell.

　　　　·　　·　　·　　·

Now like all others of her ilk, the lady had a
　　friend,
And what she made by way of trade, she gave to
　　him to spend ;
To stake him in a poker game, or pay his bar-
　　room score :

He was a pimp from Paris, and his name was Lew
    Lamore.

And so as Dooleyvitch went forth and worked as
    he was bid,
And wrested from the frozen muck the yellow
    stuff it hid,
And brought it to his Lady Nell, she gave him
    love galore—
But handed over all her gains to festive Lew
    Lamore.

      .   .   .   .   .

A year had gone, a weary year of strain and
    bloody sweat ;
Of pain and hurt in dark and dirt, of fear that she
    forget.
He sought once more her cabin door : " I've
    laboured like a beast ;
But now, dear one, the time has come to go
    before the priest.

" I've brought you gold—a hundred-fold I'll
    bring you by-and-by ;
But Oh I want you, want you bad ; I want you
    till I die.

Come, quit this life with evil rife—we'll joy
 while yet we can. . . ."
" I may not wed with you," she said ; " I love
 another man.

" I love him and I hate him so. He holds me in
 a spell.
He beats me—see my bruiséd breast ; he makes
 my life a hell.
He bleeds me, as by sin and shame I earn my
 daily bread :
Oh cruel Fate, I cannot mate till Lew Lamore
 be dead ! "

  . . . . .

The long, lean flume streaked down the hill, five
 hundred feet of fall ;
The waters in the dam above chafed at their
 prison wall ;
They surged and swept, they churned and leapt,
 with savage glee and strife ;
With spray and spume the dizzy flume thrilled
 like a thing of life.

" We must be free," the waters cried, and scur-
 ried down the slope ;

" No power can hold us back," they roared, and
    hurried in their hope.
Into a mighty pipe they plunged ; like maddened
    steers they ran,
And crashed out through a shard of steel—to
    serve the will of Man.

And there, hydraulicing his ground beside a
    bed-rock ditch,
With eye aflame and savage aim was Riley
    Dooleyvitch.
In long hip-boots and overalls, and dingy denim
    shirt,
Behind a giant monitor he pounded at the dirt.

A steely shaft of water shot, and smote the face
    of clay ;
It burrowed in the frozen muck, and scooped the
    dirt away ;
It gored the gravel from its bed, it bellowed like
    a bull ;
It hurled the heavy rocks aloft like heaps of
    fleecy wool.

Strength of a hundred men was there, resistless
    might and·skill,
And only Riley Dooleyvitch to swing it at his will.
He played it up, he played it down, nigh deafened
    by its roar,
'Till suddenly he raised his eyes, and there stood
    Lew Lamore.

Pig-eyed and heavy jowled he stood, and puffed
    a big cigar ;
As cool as though he ruled the roost in some
    Montmartre bar.
He seemed to say : " I've got a cinch, a double
    diamond hitch :
I'll skin this Muscovitish oaf, this Riley Dooley-
    vitch."

He shouted : " Stop ze water gun ; it stun me
    . . . *Sacre dam !*
I like to make one beezness deal ; you know ze
    man I am.
Zat leetle girl, she love me so—I tell you what I
    do :
You geeve to me zees claim. . . . *Jeezcrize !* I
    geeve zat girl to you."

" I'll see you damned," says Dooleyvitch ; but
    e'er he checked his tongue,
(It *may* have been an accident) the " Little
    Giant " swung ;
Swift as a lightning flash it swung, until it
    plumply bore
And met with an obstruction in the shape of Lew
    Lamore.

It caught him up, and spun him round, and
    tossed him like a ball ;
It played and pawed him in the air, before it let
    him fall.
Then just to show what it could do, with savage
    rend and thud,
It ripped the entrails from his spine, and dropped
    him in the mud.

They gathered up the broken bones, and sadly in
    a sack,
They bore to town the last remains of Lew
    Lamore, the *macque*.
And would you hear the full details of how it all befel,
Ask Missis Riley Dooleyvitch (late Touch-the-
    Button Nell).

ATOL

THE woes of men beyond my ken
Mean nothing more to me.
Behold my world, an Eden hurled
From Heaven to the Sea ;
A jewelled home, in fending foam
Tempestuously tossed ;
A virgin isle none dare defile,
Far-flung, forgotten, lost.

And here I dwell, where none may tell
Me tales of mortal strife ;
Let millions die, immune am I,
And radiant with life.
No echo comes of evil drums,
To vex my dawns divine ;
Aloof, alone I hold my throne,
And Majesty is mine.

Ghost ships pass by, and glad am I

They make no sign to me.
The green corn springs, the gilt vine clings,
The net is in the sea.
My paradise around me lies,
Remote from wrath and wrong ;
My isle is clean, unsought, unseen,
And innocent with song.

Here let me dwell in beauty's spell,
As tranquil as a tree ;
Here let me bide, where wind and tide
Bourdon that I am free ;
Here let me know from human woe
The rapture of release :
The rich caress of Loveliness,
The plenitude of Peace.

THE BALLAD OF THE ICE-WORM COCKTAIL

To Dawson Town came Percy Brown from
    London on the Thames.
A pane of glass was in his eye, and stockings on
    his stems.
Upon the shoulder of his coat a leather pad he
    wore,
To rest his deadly rifle when it wasn't seeking
    gore ;
The which it must have often been, for Major
    Percy Brown,
According to his story was a hunter of renown,
Who in the Murrumbidgee wilds had stalked the
    kangeroo
And killed the cassowary on the plains of Tim-
    buctoo.
And now the Arctic fox he meant to follow to its
    lair,

And it was also his intent to beard the Arctic
    hare. . . .
Which facts concerning Major Brown I merely
    tell because
I fain would have you know him for the Nimrod
    that he was.

Now Skipper Grey and Deacon White were
    sitting in the shack,
And sampling of the whisky that pertained to
    Sheriff Black.
Said Skipper Grey : " I want to say a word
    about this Brown :
The piker's sticking out his chest as if he owned
    the town."
Said Sheriff Black : " He has no lack of frigor-
    ated cheek ;
He called himself a Sourdough when he'd just
    been here a week."
Said Deacon White : " Methinks you're right,
    and so I have a plan
By which I hope to prove to-night the mettle of
    the man.
Just meet me where the hooch-bird sings, and
    though our ways be rude

We'll make a *proper* Sourdough of this Piccadilly
    dude."

Within the Malamute Saloon were gathered all
    the gang ;
The fun was fast and furious, and loud the hooch-
    bird sang.
In fact the night's hilarity had almost reached its
    crown,
When into its storm-centre breezed the gallant
    Major Brown.
And at the apparition, with its glass eye and plus-
    fours,
From fifty alcoholic throats resounded fifty roars.
With shouts of stark amazement and with whoops
    of sheer delight,
They surged around the stranger, but the first
    was Deacon White.
" We welcome you," he cried aloud, " to this the
    Great White Land.
The Arctic Brotherhood is proud to grip you by
    the hand.
Yea, sportsman of the bull-dog breed, from trails
    of far away,
To Yukoners this is indeed a memorable day.

Our jubilation to express, vocabularies fail. . . .
Boys, hail the Great Cheechaco!" And the boys
    responded : " Hail ! "

" And now," continued Deacon White to blush-
    ing Major Brown,
" Behold assembled the *eelight* and cream of
    Dawson Town.
And one ambition fills their hearts and makes
    their bosoms glow—
They want to make you, honoured sir, a *bony
    feed* Sourdough.
The same, some say, is one who's seen the Yukon
    ice go out,
But most profound authorities the definition
    doubt.
And to the genial notion of this meeting, Major
    Brown,
A Sourdough is a guy who drinks . . . an ice-worm
    cocktail down."

" By Gad ! " responded Major Brown, " that's
    ripping, don't you know.
I've always felt I'd like to be a *certified* Sour-
    dough.

And though I haven't any doubt your Winter's
    awf'ly nice,
Mayfair, I fear, may miss me ere the break-up of
    your ice.
Yet (pray excuse my ignorance of matters such as
    these)
A cocktail I can understand — but what's an ice-
    worm, please ? "

Said Deacon White : " It is not strange that you
    should fail to know,
Since ice-worms are peculiar to the Mountain of
    Blue Snow.
Within the Polar rim it rears, a solitary
    peak,
And in the smoke of early Spring (a spectacle
    unique)
Like flame it leaps upon the sight and thrills you
    through and through,
For though its cone is piercing white, its base is
    blazing blue.
Yet all is clear as you draw near—for coyly
    peering out
Are hosts and hosts of tiny worms, each indigo of
    snout.

And as no nourishment they find, to keep them-
    selves alive
They masticate each other's tails, till just the
    Tough survive.
Yet on this stern and Spartan fare so rapidly they
    grow,
That some attain six inches by the melting of the
    snow.
Then when the tundra glows to green and nigger-
    heads appear,
They burrow down and are not seen until another
    year.

" A toughish yarn," laughed Major Brown, " As
    well you may admit.
I'd like to see this little beast before I swallow
    it."
" 'Tis easy done," said Deacon White. " Ho !
    Barman, haste and bring
Us forth some pickled ice-worms of the vintage
    of last Spring."
But sadly still was Barman Bill, then sighed as
    one bereft :
" There's been a run on cocktails, Boss ; there
    ain't an ice-worm left.

Yet wait. . . . By gosh ! it seems to me that some
    of extra size
Were picked and put away to show the scientific
    guys."

Then deeply in a drawer he sought, and there he
    found a jar,
The which with due and proper pride he put
    upon the bar ;
And in it, wreathed in queasy rings, or rolled into
    a ball,
A score of grey and greasy things were drowned
    in alcohol.
Their bellies were a bilious blue, their eyes a
    bulbous red ;
Their backs were grey, and gross were they, and
    hideous of head.
And when with gusto and a fork the barman
    speared one out,
It must have gone four inches from its tail-tip to
    its snout.
Cried Deacon White with deep delight : " Say,
    isn't that a beaut ? "
" I think it is," sniffed Major Brown, " a most
    disgustin' brute.

Its very sight gives me the pip. I'll bet my bally
    hat,
You're only spoofin' me, old chap. You'll never
    swallow that."
" The hell I won't ! " said Deacon White. " Hey!
    Bill, that fellow's fine.
Fix up four ice-worm cocktails, and just put
    that wop in mine."

So Barman Bill got busy, and with sacerdotal air
His art's supreme achievement he proceeded to
    prepare.
His silver cups, like sickle moon, went waving to
    and fro,
And four celestial cocktails soon were shining in
    a row.
And in the starry depths of each, artistically piled,
A fat and juicy ice-worm raised its mottled mug
    and smiled.
Then closer pressed the peering crowd, suspended
    was the fun,
As Skipper Grey in courteous way said :
    " Stranger, please take one."
But with a gesture of disgust the Major shook his
    head.

E

" You can't bluff me.   You'll never drink that
    ghastly thing," he said.
" You'll see all right," said Deacon White, and
    held his cocktail high,
Till its ice-worm seemed to wiggle, and to wink a
    wicked eye.
Then Skipper Grey and Sheriff Black each lifted
    up a glass,
While through the tense and quiet crowd a
    tremor seemed to pass.
" Drink, Stranger, drink," boomed Deacon
    White.   " Proclaim you're of the best,
A doughty Sourdough who has passed the Ice-
    Worm Cocktail Test."
And at these words, with all eyes fixed on gaping
    Major Brown,
Like a libation to the gods, each dashed his
    cocktail down.

The Major gasped with horror as the trio smacked
    their lips.
He twiddelled at his eye-glass with unsteady
    finger-tips.
Into his starry cocktail with a look of woe he
    peered,

And its ice-worm, to his thinking, most incon-
tinently leered.

Yet on him were a hundred eyes, though no one
spoke aloud,

For hushed with expectation was the waiting,
watching crowd.

The Major's fumbling hand went forth—the
gang prepared to cheer ;

The Major's falt'ring hand went back, the mob
prepared to jeer.

The Major gripped his gleaming glass and laid
it to his lips,

And as despairfully he took some nauseated sips,

From out its coil of crapulence the ice-worm
raised its head ;

Its muzzle was a murky blue, its eyes a ruby red.

And then a roughneck bellowed forth : " This
stiff comes here and struts,

As if he'd bought the blasted North—jest let him
show his guts."

And with a roar the mob proclaimed : " Chee-
chako, Major Brown,

Reveal that you're of Sourdough stuff, and drink
your cocktail down."

The Major took another look, then quickly closed
    his eyes,

For even as he raised his glass he felt his gorge arise.

Aye, even though his sight was sealed, in fancy
    he could see

That grey and greasy thing that reared and
    sneered in mockery.

Yet round him ringed the callous crowd—and
    how they seemed to gloat !

It must be done. . . . He swallowed hard. . . . The
    brute was at his throat.

He choked . . . he gulped. . . . Thank God ! at
    last he'd got the horror down.

Then from the crowd went up a roar : " Hooray
    for Sourdough Brown ! "

With shouts they raised him shoulder high, and
    gave a rousing cheer,

But though they praised him to the sky the
    Major did not hear.

Amid their demonstrative glee delight he seemed
    to lack ;

Indeed it almost seemed that he—was " keeping
    something back."

A clammy sweat was on his brow, and pallid as
    a sheet :

"I feel I must be going now," he'd plaintively
    repeat.
Aye, though with drinks and smokes galore, they
    tempted him to stay,
With sudden bolt he gained the door, and made
    his get-a-way.

And ere next night his story was the talk of
    Dawson Town,
But gone and reft of glory was the wrathful
    Major Brown ;
For that ice-worm (so they told him) of such
    formidable size
Was—*a stick of stained spaghetti with two red ink
    spots for eyes.*

GRANDAD

HEAVEN's mighty sweet, I guess ;
Ain't no rush to git there ;
Been a sinner, more or less ;
Maybe wouldn't fit there.
Wicked still, bound to confess ;
Might jest pine a bit there.

Heaven's swell, the preachers say :
Got so used to earth here ;
Had such good times all the way,
Frolic, fun and mirth here ;
Eighty Springs ago to-day,
Since I had my birth here.

Quite a spell of happy years.
Wish I could begin it ;
Cloud and sunshine, laughter, tears,
Livin' every minute.
Women, too, the pretty dears ;
Plenty of 'em in it.

Heaven ! that's another tale.
Mightn't let me chew there.
Gotta have me pot of ale ;
Would I like the brew there ?
Maybe I'd get slack and stale —
No more chores to do there.

Here I weed the garden plot,
Scare the crows from pillage ;
Simmer in the sun a lot,
Talk about the tillage.
Yarn of battles I have fought,
Greybeard of the village.

Heaven's mighty fine, I know. . . .
Still, it ain't so bad here.
See them maples all aglow ;
Starlings seem so glad here :
I'll be mighty peeved to go,
Scrumptious times I've had here.

Lord, I know You'll understand.
With Your Light You'll lead me.
Though I'm not the pious brand,
I'm here when you need me.
Gosh ! I know that Heaven's GRAND,
But dang it ! God, *don't speed me.*

THE BALLAD OF THE LEATHER MEDAL

ONLY a Leather Medal, hanging there on the
  wall,
Dingy and frayed and faded, dusty and worn and
  old ;
Yet of my humble treasures I value it most of all,
And I wouldn't part with that medal if you gave
  me its weight in gold.

Read the inscription : *For Valour—presented to
  Millie MacGee*.
Ah ! how in mem'ry it takes me back to the " auld
  lang syne,"
When Millie and I were sweethearts, and fair as
  a flower was she—
Yet little I dreamt that her bosom held the heart
  of a heroine.

Listen ! I'll tell you about it. . . . An orphan
  was Millie MacGee,

Living with Billie her brother, under the Yukon
    sky.
Sam, her pa, was cremated in the winter of
    nineteen-three,
As duly and truly related by the pen of an author
    guy.

A cute little kid was Billie, solemn and silken of
    hair,
The image of Jackie Coogan in the days before
    movies could speak.
Devoted to him was Millie, with more than a
    mother's care,
And happy were they together in their cabin on
    Bunker Creek.

'Twas only a mining village, where hearts are
    simple and true,
And Millie MacGee was schoolma'am, loved and
    admired by all ;
Yet no one dreamed for a moment she'd do what
    she dared to do—
But wait and I'll try to tell you, as clear as I can
    recall. . . .

    .   .   .   .   .

Christmas Eve in the school-house ! A scene of
    glitter and glee ;
The children eager and joyful ; parents and
    neighbours too ;
Right in the forefront, Millie, close to the
    Christmas Tree,
While Billie, her brother, recited " The Shooting
    of Dan McGrew."

I reckon you've heard the opus, a ballad of guts
    and gore ;
Of a Yukon frail and a frozen trail and a fight in
    a drinking dive.
It's on a par, I figger, with " The Face on the
    Bar Room Floor,"
And the boys who wrote them pieces ought to be
    skinned alive.

Picture that scene of gladness : the honest faces
    aglow ;
The kiddies gaping and spellbound, as Billie
    strutted his stuff.
The stage with its starry candles, and there in the
    foremost row,

Millie, bright as a fairy, in radiant flounce and
    fluff.

More like an angel I thought her ; all she needed
    was wings,
And I sought for a smile seraphic, but her eyes
    were only for Bill ;
So there was I longing and loving, and dreaming
    the craziest things,
And Billie shouting and spouting, and everyone
    rapt and still.

Proud as a prince was Billie, bang in the foot-
    lights' glare,
And quaking for him was Millie, as she followed
    every word ;
Then just as he reached the climax, ranting and
    sawing the air—
Ugh ! How it makes me shudder ! The horrible
    thing occurred. . . .

"Twas the day when frocks were frilly, and skirts
    were scraping the ground,
And the snowy flounces of Millie like sea foam
    round her swept ;

Humbly adoring I watched her—when oh, my
    heart gave a bound !
Hoary and scarred and hideous, out from the
    tree . . . IT . . . crept.

A whiskered, beady-eyed monster, grisly and
    grim of hue ;
Savage and slinking and silent, born of the dark
    and the dirt ;
Dazed by the glare and the glitter, it wavered a
    moment or two—
Then like a sinister shadow, it vanished . . .
    'neath Millie's skirt.

I stared. Had my eyes deceived me ? I shivered.
    I held my breath.
Surely I must have dreamed it ? I quivered. I
    made to rise. . . .
Then—my God ! it was real. Millie grew pale
    as death ;
And oh, such a look of terror woke in her lovely
    eyes.

Did her scream ring out ? Ah no, sir. It froze
    at her very lips.

Clenching her teeth she checked it, and I saw
    her slim hands lock,
Grasping and gripping tensely, with desperate
    finger tips,
Something that writhed and wriggled under her
    dainty frock.

Quick I'd have dashed to her rescue, but fiercely
    she signalled : " No ! "
Her eyes were dark with anguish, but her lips
    were set and grim ;
Then I knew she was thinking of Billie—the
    kiddy must have his show,
Reap to the full his glory, nothing mattered but
    him.

So spiked to my chair with horror, there I shud-
    dered and saw
Her fingers frenziedly clutching and squeezing
    with all their might
Something that squirmed and struggled, a demon
    of tooth and claw,
Fighting with fear and fury, under her garment
    white.

Oh could I only aid her ! But the wide room lay
    between,
And again her eyes besought me : " Steady ! "
    they seemed to say.
" Stay where you are, Bob Simmons ; don't let
    us have a scene.
Billie will soon be finished. Only a moment . . .
    stay ! "

A moment ! Ah yes, I got her. I knew how
    night after night
She'd learned him each line of that ballad with
    patience and pride and glee ;
With gesture and tone dramatic, she'd taught him
    how to recite. . . .
And now at the last to fail him—no, it must
    never be.

A moment ! It seemed like ages. Why was
    Billie so slow ?
He stammered. Twice he repeated : " The
    Lady that's known as Lou——"
The kiddy was stuck and she knew it. Her face
    was frantic with woe.

Could she but come to his rescue ? Could she
    remember the cue ?

I saw her whispering wildly as she leaned to the
    frightened boy ;
But Billie stared like a dummy, and I stifled an
    anxious curse.
Louder, louder she prompted ; then his face
    illumined with joy,
And panting, flushed and exultant, he finished
    the final verse.

So the youngster wound up like a whirlwind,
    while cheer resounded on cheer ;
His piece was the hit of the evening. " Bravo ! "
    I heard them say.
But there in the heart of the racket was one who
    could not hear—
The loving sister who'd coached him ; for Millie
    had fainted away.

I rushed to her side and grabbed her ; then
    others saw her distress,
And all were eager to aid me, as I pillowed that
    golden head.

But her arms were tense and rigid, and clutched
    in the folds of her dress,
Unlocking her hands they found it . . . A RAT . . .
    and the brute was dead.

In silence she'd crushed its life out, rather than
    scare the crowd,
And queer little Billie's triumph. . . . Hey!
    Mother, what about tea?
I've just been telling a story that makes me so
    mighty proud. . . .
Stranger, let me present you—*my wife, that was
    Millie MacGee.*

COURAGE

To-day I opened wide my eyes,
And stared with wonder and surprise,
To see beneath November skies
An apple blossom peer ;
Upon a branch as bleak as night
It gleamed exultant on my sight,
A fairy beacon burning bright
Of hope and cheer.

" Alas ! " said I, " poor foolish thing,
Have you mistaken this for Spring ?
Behold, the thrush has taken wing,
And Winter's near."
`Serene it seemed to lift its head :
" The Winter's wrath I do not dread,
Because I am," it proudly said,
" A Pioneer.

" Some apple-blossom must be first,

With beauty's urgency to burst
Into a world for joy athirst,
And so I dare ;
And I shall see what none shall see—
December skies gloom over me,
And mock them with my April glee,
And fearless fare.

" And I shall hear what none shall hear—
The hardy robin piping clear,
The Storm King gallop dark and drear
Across the sky ;
And I shall know what none shall know—
The silent kisses of the snow,
The Christmas candles' silver glow,
Before I die.

" Then from your frost-gemmed window pane
One morning you will look in vain,
My smile of delicate disdain
No more to see ;
But though I pass before my time,
And perish in the grale and grime,
Maybe you'll have a little rhyme
To spare for me."

A SOURDOUGH STORY

Hark to a Sourdough story, told at sixty below,
When the pipes are lit and we smoke and spit
Into the campfire glow.
Rugged are we and hoary, and statin' a general
*   rule,*
A genooine Sourdough story
Ain't no yarn for the Sunday School.

A Sourdough came to stake his claim in Heav'n
    one morning early.
Saint Peter cried : " Who waits outside them
    gates so bright and pearly ? "
" I'm recent dead," the Sourdough said, " and
    crave to visit Hades,
Where haply pine some pals o' mine, includin'
    certain ladies."
Said Peter : " Go, you old Sourdough, from life
    so crooly riven ;
And if ye fail to find their trail, we'll have a snoop
    round Heaven."

83

He waved, and lo ! that old Sourdough dropped
 down to Hell's red spaces ;
But though 'twas hot he couldn't spot them old
 familiar faces.
The bedrock burned, and so he turned, and
 climbed with footsteps fleeter,
The stairway straight to Heaven's gate, and there,
 of course, was Peter.
" I cannot see my mates," sez he, " among those
 damned forever.
I have a hunch some of the bunch in Heaven I'll
 discover."
Said Peter : " True ;   and this I'll do (since
 Sourdoughs are my failing)
You see them guys in Paradise, lined up against
 the railing—
As bald as coots, in *birthday* suits, with beards
 below the middle . . .
Well, I'll allow you in right now, if you can solve
 a riddle :
Among that gang of stiffs who hang and dodder
 round the portals,
Is one whose name is known to Fame—it's Adam,
 first of mortals.

For quiet's sake he makes a break from Eve,
    which is his Madame. . . .
Well, there's the gate.—To crash it straight, just
    spy the guy that's Adam."

The old Sourdough went down the row of grey-
    beards ruminatin'.
With optics dim they peered at him, and pressed
    agin the gratin'.
In every face he sought some trace of our ances-
    tral father ;
But though he stared, he soon despaired the
    faintest clue to gather.
Then suddenly he whooped with glee : " Ha !
    Ha ! an inspiration."
And to and fro along the row he ran with anima-
    tion.
To Peter, bold he cried : " Behold, all told there
    are eleven.
Suppose I fix on Number Six—say Boy ! How's
    that for Heaven ? "

" By Gosh ! you win," said Pete, " Step in. But
    tell me how you chose him.

They're like as pins ; all might be twins. There's
    nothing to disclose him."

The Sourdough said : " 'Twas hard ; my head
    was seething with commotion.

I felt a dunce ; then all at once I had a gorgeous
    notion.

I stooped and peered beneath each beard that
    drooped like fleece of mutton.

My search was crowned. . . . That bird I found—
    ain't got no belly button."

ALOUETTE

SINGING larks I saw for sale —
(Ah ! the pain of it)
Plucked and ready to impale
On the roasting spit ;
Happy larks that summer-long
Stormed the radiant sky,
Adoration in their song . . .
Packed to make a pie.

Hark ! from springs of joy unseen
Spray their jewelled notes.
Tangle them in nets of green,
Twist their lyric throats ;
Clip their wings and string them tight,
Stab them with a skewer,
All to tempt the appetite
Of the epicure.

Shade of Shelley ! Come not nigh

This accursed spot,
Where for sixpence one can buy
Skylarks for the pot ;
Dante, paint a blacker hell,
Plunge in deeper darks
Wretches who can slay and sell
Sunny-hearted larks.

You who eat, you are the worst :
By internal pains,
May you ever be accurst
Who pluck these poor remains.
But for you winged joy would soar
To heaven from the sod :
In ecstasy a lark would pour
Its gratitude to God.

THE BALLAD OF LENIN'S TOMB

This is the yarn he told to me
As we sat in Casey's Bar,
That Rooshun mug who scrammed from the jug
In the Land of the Crimson Star ;
That Soveet guy with the single eye,
And the face like a flaming scar.

WHERE Lenin lies the red flag flies, and rat-grey
  workers wait
To tread the gloom of Lenin's Tomb, where the
  Comrade lies in state.
With lagging pace they scan his face, so weary
  yet so firm ;
For years a score they've laboured sore to save
  him from the worm.
The Kremlin walls are grimly grey, but Lenin's
  Tomb is red,
And pilgrims from the Sour Lands say : " He
  sleeps and is not dead."

Before their eyes in peace he lies, a symbol and
    a sign,

And as they pass that dome of glass they see—a
    God Divine.

So Doctors plug him full of dope, for if he drops
    to dust,

So will collapse their faith and hope, the whole
    combine will bust.

But stay, Tovarich ; hark to me . . . a secret I'll
    disclose,

For I did see what none did see ; I know what
    no one knows.

I was a Cheko terrorist—Oh I served the Soviets
    well,

Till they put me down on the bone-yard list, for
    the fear that I might tell ;

That I might tell the thing I saw, and that only I
    did see,

They held me in quod with a firing squad to
    make a corpse of me.

But I got away, and here to-day I'm telling my
    tale to you ;

Though it may sound weird, by Lenin's beard,
    so help me God it's true.

I slouched across the great Red Square, and
    watched the waiting line.

The mongrel sons of Marx were there, convened
    to Lenin's shrine ;

Ten thousand men of Muscovy, Mongol and
    Turkoman,

Black-bonnets of the Aral Sea and Tatars of Kazan.

Kalmuck and Bashkir, Lett and Finn, Georgian,
    Jew and Lapp,

Kirghis and Kazakh, crowding in to gaze on
    Lenin's map.

Aye, though a score of years had run I saw them
    pause and pray,

As mourners at the Tomb of one who died but
    yesterday.

I watched them in a bleary daze of bitterness and
    pain,

For oh, I missed the cheery blaze of vodka in my
    brain.

I stared, my eyes were hypnotized by that satur-
    nine host,

When with a start that shook my heart I saw—I
    saw a ghost.

As in fogged glass I saw him pass, and peer at
    me and grin—

A man I knew, a man I *slew*, Prince Boris
Mazarin.

Now do not think because I drink I love the
flowing bowl ;
But liquor kills remorse and stills the anguish of
the soul.
And there's so much I would forget, stark horrors
I have seen,
Faces and forms that haunt me yet, like shadows
on a screen.
And of these sights that mar my nights the
ghastliest by far
Is the death of Boris Mazarin, that soldier of the
Czar.

A mighty nobleman was he ; we took him by
surprise ;
His mother, son and daughters three we slew
before his eyes.
We tortured him, with jibes and threats ; then
mad for glut of gore,
Upon our reeking bayonets we nailed him to the
door.

But he defied us to the last, crying : " O carrion
    crew !
I'd die with joy could I destroy a hundred dogs
    like you."
I thrust my sword into his throat ; the blade was
    gay with blood ;
We flung him to his castle moat, and stamped him
    in its mud.
That mighty Cossack of the Don was dead with
    all his race. . . .
And now I saw him coming on, dire vengeance
    in his face.
(Or was it some fantastic dream of my besotted
    brain ?)
He looked at me with eyes a-gleam, the man
    whom I had slain.
He looked and bade me follow him ; I could not
    help but go ;
I joined the throng that passed along, so sorrow-
    ful and slow.
I followed with a sense of doom that shadow
    gaunt and grim ;
Into the bowels of the Tomb I followed, followed
    him.

The light within was weird and dim, and icy cold
    the air ;
My brow was wet with bitter sweat, I stumbled
    on the stair.
I tried to cry ; my throat was dry ; I sought to
    grip his arm ;
For well I knew this man I slew was there to do
    us harm.
Lo ! he was walking by my side, his fingers
    clutched my own,
This man I knew so well had died, his hand was
    naked bone.
His face was like a skull, his eyes were caverns of
    decay . . .
And so we came to the crystal frame where
    lonely Lenin lay.

Without a sound we shuffled round. I sought to
    make a sign,
But like a vice his hand of ice was biting into
    mine.
With leaden pace around the place where Lenin
    lies at rest,
We slouched, I saw his bony claw go fumbling
    to his breast.

With ghastly grin he groped within, and tore his
    robe apart,
And from the hollow of his ribs he drew his
    blackened heart. . . .
Ah no! Oh God! A *bomb*, a BOMB! And as I
    shrieked with dread,
With fiendish cry he raised it high, and . . . swung
    at Lenin's head.

Oh I was blinded by the flash and deafened by
    the roar,
And in a mess of bloody mash I wallowed on the
    floor.
Then Alps of darkness on me fell, and when I
    saw again
The leprous light 'twas in a cell, and I was racked
    with pain ;
And ringed around by shapes of gloom, who
    hoped that I would die ;
For of the crowd that crammed the Tomb the
    sole to live was I.
They told me I had dreamed a dream that must
    not be revealed,
But by their eyes of evil gleam I knew my doom
    was sealed.

I need not tell how from my cell in Lubianka
    gaol,
I broke away, but listen, here's the point of all
    my tale. . . .
Outside the " Gay Pay Oo " none knew of that
    grim scene of gore ;
They closed the Tomb, and then they threw it
    open as before.
And there was Lenin, stiff and still, a symbol and
    a sign,
And rancid races come to thrill and wonder at his
    Shrine ;
And hold the thought : if Lenin rot the Soviets
    will decay ;
So there he sleeps and calm he keeps his watch
    and ward for aye.

Yet if you pass that frame of glass, peer closely at
    his phiz,
So stern and firm it mocks the worm, it looks like
    wax . . . *and is*.
They tell you he's a mummy—don't you make
    that bright mistake :
I tell you—he's a dummy ; aye, a fiction and a
    fake.

This *eye* beheld the bloody bomb that bashed
    him on the bean.
I heard the crash, I saw the flash, yet . . . . there
    he lies serene.
And by the roar that rocked the Tomb I ask :
    how could that be ?
But if you doubt that deed of doom, just go
    yourself and see.
You think I'm mad, or drunk, or both. . . . Well,
    I don't care a damn :
I tell you this : their Lenin is a waxen, show-case
    SHAM.

Such was the yarn he handed me,
Down there in Casey's Bar,
That Rooshun bug with the scrambled mug
From the Land of the Commissar.
It may be true, I leave it you
To figger out how far.

G

MAIDS IN MAY

THREE maids there were in meadow bright,
The eldest less than seven ;
Their eyes were dancing with delight,
And innocent as Heaven.

Wild flowers they wound with tender glee,
Their cheeks with rapture rosy ;
All radiant they smiled at me,
When I besought a posy.

So one gave me a columbine,
And one a poppy brought me ;
The tiniest, with eyes ashine,
A simple daisy sought me.

And as I went my sober way,
I heard their careless laughter ;
Their hearts too happy with to-day
To care for what comes after.

.   .   .   .   .

That's long ago ; they're gone, all three,
To walk amid the shadows ;
Forgotten is their lyric glee
In still and sunny meadows.

For Columbine loved life too well
And went adventure faring ;
And sunk into the pit of hell,
And passed but little caring.

While Poppy was a poor man's wife,
And children had a-plenty ;
And went, worn out with toil and strife
When she was five-and-twenty.

And Daisy died while yet a child,
As fragile blossoms perish,
When Winter winds are harsh and wild,
With none to shield and cherish.

*Ah me ! How Fate is dark and dour
To little Children of the Poor.*

THE BALLAD OF CASEY'S BILLY-GOAT

You've heard of " Casey at The Bat,"
And " Casey's Tabble Dote " ;
But now it's time
To write the rhyme
Of " Casey's Billy-goat."

PAT CASEY had a billy-goat he gave the name of
Shamus,
Because it was (the neighbours said) a national
disgrace.
And sure enough that animal was eminently
famous
For masticating every rag of laundry round the
place.
From shirts to skirts prodigiously it proved its
powers of chewing ;
The question of digestion seemed to matter not
at all ;

But you'll agree, I think with me, its limit of
    mis-doing
Was reached the day it swallowed Missis Rooney's
    ould red shawl.

Now Missis Annie Rooney was a winsome widow
    woman,
And many a bouncing boy had sought to make
    her change her name ;
And living just across the way 'twas surely only
    human
A lonesome man like Casey should be wishfully
    the same.
So every Sunday, shaved and shined, he'd make
    the fine occasion
To call upon the lady, and she'd take his hat and
    coat ;
And supping tea it seemed that she might yield
    to his persuasion,
But alas ! he hadn't counted on that devastating
    goat.

For Shamus loved his master with a deep and
    dumb devotion,

And everywhere that Casey went that goat would
    want to go ;
And though I cannot analyse a quadruped's
    emotion,
They said the baste was jealous, and I reckon it
    was so.
For every time that Casey went to call on Missis
    Rooney,
Beside the gate the goat would wait with woeful-
    ness intense ;
Until one day it chanced that they were fast
    becoming spooney,
When Shamus spied that ould red shawl a-flutter
    on the fence.

Now Missis Rooney loved that shawl beyond all
    rhyme or reason,
And maybe 'twas an heirloom or a cherished
    souvenir ;
For judging by the way she wore it season after
    season,
It might have been as precious as a product of
    Cashmere.
So Shamus strolled towards it, and no doubt the
    colour pleased him,

For he biffed it and he sniffed it, as most any
    goat might do ;
Then his melancholy vanished as a sense of
    hunger seized him,
And he wagged his tail with rapture as he started
    in to chew.

" Begorrah ! you're a daisy," said the doting
    Mister Casey
To the blushing Widow Rooney as they parted
    at the door.
" Wid yer tinderness an' tazin' sure ye've set me
    heart a-blazin',
And I dread the day I'll nivver see me Annie
    anny more."
" Go on now wid yer blarney," said the widow
    softly sighing ;
And she went to pull his whiskers, when dismay
    her bosom smote. . . .
Her ould red shawl ! 'Twas missin' where she'd
    left it bravely drying—
Then she saw it disappearing—down the neck of
    Casey's goat.

Fiercely flamed her Irish temper. " Look ! "
    says she, " The thavin' divvle !

Sure he's made me shawl his supper. Well, I
      hope it's to his taste ;
But excuse me, Mister Casey, if I seem to be
      oncivil,
For I'll nivver wed a man wid such a mis-
      begotten baste."
So she slammed the door and left him in a state
      of consternation,
And he couldn't understand it, till he saw that
      grinning goat ;
Then with eloquence he cussed it, and his final
      fulmination
Was a poem of profanity impossible to quote.

So blasting goats and petticoats, and feeling
      downright sinful,
Despairfully he wandered in to Shinnigan's she-
      been ;
And straightway he proceeded to absorb a
      mighty skinful
Of the deadliest variety of Shinnigan's potheen.
And when he started homeward it was in the
      early morning,
But Shamus followed faithfully, a yard behind
      his back ;

Then Casey slipped and stumbled, and without
    the slightest warning
Like a lump of lead he tumbled—right across the
    railway track.

And there he lay, serenely, and defied the powers
    to budge him,
Reposing like a baby, with his head upon a rail ;
But Shamus seemed unhappy, and from time to
    time would nudge him,
Though his prods of protestation were without
    the least avail.
Then to that goatish mind, maybe, a sense of
    fell disaster
Came stealing like a spectre in the dim and
    dreary dawn ;
For his bleat of warning blended with the snoring
    of his master
In a chorus of calamity—but Casey slumbered
    on.

Yet oh, that goat was troubled, for his efforts
    were redoubled ;
Now he tugged at Casey's whisker, now he
    nibbled at his ear ;

Now he shook him by the shoulder, and with
    fear becoming bolder,
He bellowed like a fog-horn, but the sleeper did
    not hear.
Then up and down the railway line he scampered
    for assistance ;
But anxiously he hurried back and sought with
    tug and strain
To pull his master off the track . . . when sudden !
    in the distance
He heard the roar and rumble of the fast ap-
    proaching train.

Did Shamus faint and falter ? No, he stood there
    stark and splendid.
True, his tummy was distended, but he gave his
    horns a toss.
By them his goathood's honour would be gal-
    lantly defended,
And if their valour failed him—he would perish
    with his boss.
So dauntlessly he lowered his head, and ever
    clearer, clearer,
He heard the throb and thunder of the Conti-
    nental Mail.

He would face that mighty monster. It was
    coming nearer, nearer ;
He would fight it, he would smite it, but he'd
    never show his tail.

Can you see that hirsute hero, standing there in
    tragic glory ?
Can you hear the Pullman porters shrieking
    horror to the sky ?
No, you can't ; because my story has no end so
    grim and gory,
For Shamus did not perish and his master did
    not die.
At this very present moment Casey swaggers hale
    and hearty,
And Shamus strolls beside him with a bright bell
    at his throat ;
While the recent Missis Rooney is the gayest of
    the party,
For now she's Missis Casey and she's crazy for
    that goat.

You're wondering what happened ? Well, you
    know that truth is stranger

Than the wildest brand of fiction, so I'll tell you
    without shame. . . .
There was Shamus and his master in the face of
    awful danger,
And the giant locomotive dashing down in smoke
    and flame. . . .
What power on earth could save them ? Yet a
    golden inspiration
To gods and goats alike may come, so in that
    brutish brain
A thought was born—*the ould red shawl*. . . .
    Then rearing with elation,
Like lightning Shamus *threw it up*—AND
    FLAGGED AND STOPPED THE TRAIN.

THE SMOKING FROG

THREE men I saw beside a bar,
Regarding o'er their bottle,
A frog who smoked a rank cigar
They'd jammed within its throttle.

A Pasha frog it must have been,
So big it was and bloated ;
And from its lips the nicoteen
In graceful festoon floated.

And while the trio jeered and joked,
As if it quite enjoyed it,
Impassively it smoked and smoked,
(It could not well avoid it.)

A ring of fire its lips were nigh,
Yet it seemed all unwitting ;
It could not spit, like you and I,
Who've learned the art of spitting.

It did not wink, it did not shrink,
As there serene it squatted ;
Its eyes were clear, it did not fear
The fate the Gods allotted.

It squatted there with calm sublime,
Amid their cruel guying ;
Grave as a god, and all the time
It knew that it was dying.

And somehow then it seemed to me
These men expectorating,
Were infinitely less than he,
The dumb thing they were baiting.

It seemed to say, despite their jokes :
" This is my hour of glory.
It isn't every frog that smokes :
My name will live in story."

Before its nose the smoke arose ;
The flame grew nigher, nigher ;
And then I saw its bright eyes close
Beside that ring of fire.

They turned it on its warty back,
From off its bloated belly ;
Its legs jerked out, then dangled slack ;
It quivered like a jelly.

And then the fellows went away,
Contented with their joking ;
But even as in death it lay,
The frog continued smoking.

Life's like a lighted fag, thought I ;
We smoke it stale ; then after
Death turns our belly to the sky :
The Gods must have their laughter.

MADAME LA MARQUISE

SAID Hongray de le Glaciere unto his proud Papa:
" I want to take a wife, *mon Père*." The Marquis
    laughed : " Ha ! Ha !

And whose, my son ? " he slyly said ; but
    Hongray with a frown

Cried : " Fi ! Papa, I mean—to wed. I want to
    settle down."

The Marquis de la Glaciere responded with a
    smile :

" You're young, my boy ; I much prefer that
    you should wait awhile."

But Hongray sighed : " I cannot wait, for I am
    twenty-four ;

And I have met my blessed fate : I worship, I
    adore.

Such beauty, grace and charm has she, I'm sure
    you will approve,

For if I live a century none other can I love."

" I have no doubt," the Marquis shrugged, " that
    she's a proper pet ;
But has she got a decent *dot*, and is she of our
    set ? "
" Her *dot*," said Hongray, " will suffice ; her
    family you know.
The girl with whom I fain would splice is
    Mirabelle du Veau."

What made the Marquis start and stare, and
    clutch his perfumed beard ?
Why did he stagger to a chair, and murmur :
    " As I feared " ?
Dilated were his eyes with dread, and in a voice
    of woe
He wailed : " My son, you cannot wed with
    Mirabelle du Veau."
" Why not ? my Parent," Hongray cried. " Her
    name's without a slur.
Why should you look so horrified that I should
    wed with her ? "
The Marquis groaned : " Unhappy lad ! Forget
    her if you can,
And see in your respected Dad a miserable man."

H

" What is the matter ?   I repeat," said Hongray
      growing hot.
" She's witty, pretty, rich and sweet. . . . Then—
      mille diables !—what ? "
The Marquis moaned : " Alas ! that I your
      dreams of bliss should banish ;
It happened in the days gone-by, when I was
      Don Juanish.
Her mother was your mother's friend, and we
      were much together.
Ah well ! You know how such things end.   (I
      blame it on the weather.)
We had a very sultry spell.   One day, *mon Dieu !*
      I kissed her.
My son, you can't wed Mirabelle.   She is . . .
      she is your sister."

So broken-hearted Hongray went and roamed
      the world around,
Till hunting in the Occident forgetfulness he
      found.
Then quite recovered, he returned to the paternal
      nest,
Until one day, with brow that burned, the
      Marquis he addressed :

" Felicitate me, Father mine ; my brain is in a
    whirl ;
For I have found the mate divine, the one, the
    perfect girl.
She's healthy, wealthy, witching, wise, with
    loveliness serene.
Ah ! Proud am I to win a prize, half angel and
    half queen."
" 'Tis time to wed," the Marquis said. " You
    must be twenty-seven.
But who is she whose lot may be to make your
    life a heaven ? "
" A friend of childhood," Hongray cried. " For
    whom regard you feel.
The maid I fain would make my bride is Ray-
    monde de la Veal."

The Marquise de la Glaciere collapsed upon the
    floor,
And all the words he uttered were : " Forgive
    me, I implore.
My sins are heavy on my head. Profound re-
    morse I feel.
My son, you simply cannot wed with Raymonde
    de la Veal."

Then Hongray spoke with voice that broke, and
    corrugated brow :

" Inform me, Sir, why you demur. What is the
    matter now ? "

The Marquis wailed : " My wicked youth ! Ah !
    how it gives me pain.

But let me tell the awful truth, my agony
    explain. . . .

A cursed Casanova I ; a finished flirt her
    mother ;

And so alas ! it came to pass we fell for one
    another.

Our lives were blent in bliss and joy. The
    sequel you may gather :

You cannot wed Raymonde, my boy, because I
    am . . . *her father*."

Again sore-stricken Hongray fled, and sought his
    grief to smother,

And as he writhed upon his bed to him there
    came his Mother.

The Marquise de la Glaciere was snowy-haired
    and frigid.

Her wintry features chiselled were, her manner
    stiff and rigid.

The pride of race was in her face, her bearing
    high and stately,
And sinking down by Hongray's side she spoke
    to him sedately :
" What ails you so, my precious child ? What
    thongs of sorrow smite you ?
Why are your eyes so wet and wild ? Come, tell
    me, I invite you."
" Ah ! if I told you, Mother dear," said Hongray
    with a shiver,
" Another's honour would, I fear, be in the soup
    forever."
"Nay trust," she begged, "My only boy, the fond
    Mama who bore you.
Perhaps I may, your grief alloy. Please tell me,
    I implore you."

And so his story Hongray told, in accents choked
    and muffled.
The Marquise listened calm and cold, her visage
    quite unruffled.
He told of Mirabelle de Veau, his agony reveal-
    ing.
For Raymonde de la Veal his woe was quite
    beyond concealing.

And still she sat without a word, her look so high
    and haughty,
You'd ne'er have thought it was her lord who had
    behaved so naughty.
Then Hongray finished up : " For life my hopes
    are doomed to slaughter ;
For if I choose another wife, she's *sure* to be his
    daughter."

The Marquise rose. " Cheer up," said she, " the
    last word is not spoken.
A Mother cannot sit and see her boy's heart
    rudely broken.
So dry your tears and calm your fears ; no
    longer need you tarry ;
To-day your bride you may decide, to-morrow
    you may marry.
Yes, you may wed with Mirabelle, or Raymonde
    if you'd rather. . . .
For I as well the truth may tell . . . *Papa is not
    your father.*"

BEACHCOMBER

WHEN I have come with happy heart to sixty
    years and ten,
I'll buy a boat and sail away upon a summer sea ;
And in a little lonely isle that's far and far from
    men,
In peace and praise I'll spend the days the Gods
    allow to me.
For I am weary of a strife so pitiless and vain ;
And in a far and fairy isle, bewilderingly bright,
I'll learn to know the leap and glow of rapture
    once again,
And welcome every living dawn with wonder and
    delight.

And there I'll build a swan-white house above
    the singing foam,
With brooding eaves, where joyously rich roses
    climb and cling ;

With crotons in a double row, like wine and
    honeycomb,
And flame trees dripping golden rain, and palms
    pavilioning.
And there I'll let the wind and wave do what they
    will with me ;
And I will dwell unto the end with loveliness and
    joy ;
And drink from out the crystal spring, and eat
    from off the tree,
As simple as a savage is, as careless as a boy.

For I have come to think that Life's a lamentable
    tale,
And all we break our hearts to win is little worth
    our while ;
For fame and fortune in the end are comfortless
    and stale,
And it is best to dream and rest upon a radiant
    isle.
So I'll blot out the bitter years of sufferance and
    scorn,
And I'll forget the fear and fret, the poverty and
    pain ;

And in a shy and secret isle I'll be a man new-
born,
And fashion life to hearts desire, and seek my
soul again.

For when I come with happy heart to sixty year
and ten,
I fondly hope the best of life will yet remain to
me ;
And so I'll burn my foolish books and break my
futile pen,
And seek a tranced and tranquil isle, that dreams
eternally.
I'll turn my back on all the world, I'll bid my
friends adieu ;
Unto the blind I'll leave behind what gold I have
to give ;
And in a jewelled solitude I'll mould my life
anew,
And nestling close to Nature's heart, I'll learn at
last . . . to live.

JOBSON OF THE *STAR*

WITHIN a pub that's off the Strand and handy to
    the bar,
With pipe in mouth and mug in hand sat Jobson
    of the *Star*.
" Come, sit ye down, ye wand'ring wight, and
    have a yarn," says he.
" I can't," says I, " because to-night I'm off to
    Tripoli ;
To Tripoli and Trebezond and Timbuctoo may-
    hap,
Or any magic name beyond I find upon the map.
I go the errant trail to try, to clutch the skirts of
    Chance,
To make once more before I die the gesture of
    Romance."
Then Jobson yawned above his jug, and rumbled :
    " Is that so ?
Well, anyway, sit down, you mug, and drink
    before you go."

Now Jobson is a chum of mine, and in a dusty
    den,
Within the street that's known as Fleet, he wields
    a wicked pen.
And every night it's his delight, above the fleeting
    show,
To castigate the living Great, and keep the lowly
    low.
And all there is to know he knows, for unto him
    is spurred
The knowledge of the knowledge of the Thing
    That Has Occurred.
And all that is to hear he hears, for to his ear is
    whirled
The echo of the echo of the Sound That Shocks
    The World.
Let Revolutions rage and rend, and Kingdoms
    rise and fall,
There Jobson sits and smokes and spits, and
    writes about it all.

And so we jawed a little while on matters small
    and great ;
He told me with his cynic smile of grave affairs
    of state.

Of princes, peers and presidents, and folk beyond
    my ken
He spoke as you and I might speak of ordinary
    men.
For Jobson is a scribe of worth, and has respect
    for none,
And all the mighty ones of earth are targets for
    his fun.
So when I said good-bye, says he, with his
    satyric leer :
" Too bad to go, when life is so damned inter-
    esting here.
The Government rides for a fall, and things are
    getting hot.
You'd better stick around, old pal ; you'll miss
    an awful lot."

Yet still I went and wandered far, by secret ways
    and wide.
Adventure was the shining star I took to be my
    guide.
For fifty moons I followed on, and every moon
    was sweet,
And lit as if for me alone the trail before my
    feet.

From cities desolate with doom my moons swam
    up and set,
On tower and temple, tent and tomb, on mosque
    and minaret.
To heights that hailed the dawn I scaled, by cliff
    and chasm sheer ;
To far Cathay I found my way, and fabulous
    Kashmir.
From camel-back I traced the track that bars the
    barren *bled*,
And leads to hell-and-blazes, and I followed
    where it led.
Like emeralds in sapphire set, and ripe for human
    rape,
I passed with passionate regret the Islands of
    Escape.
With death I clinched a time or two, and gave the
    brute a fall.
Hunger and cold and thirst I knew, yet . . . how
    I loved it all !
Then suddenly I seemed to tire of trekking up
    and down,
And longed for some domestic fire, and sailed for
    London Town.

And in a pub that's off the Strand, and handy to
    the bar,

With pipe in mouth and mug in hand sat Jobson
    of the *Star*.

" Hullo ! " says he. " Come, take a pew, and tell
    me where you've been.

It seems to me that lately you have vanished
    from the scene."

" I've been," says I, " to Kordovan and Kong and
    Calabar,

To Sarawak and Samarkand, to Ghat and Bolivar;

To Caracas and Guyaquil, to Lhassa and Pekin,

To Bramaputra and Brazil, to Bagdad and Benin.

I've sailed the Black Sea and the White, the
    Yellow and the Red,

The Sula and the Celebes, the Behering and the
    Dead.

I've climbed on Chimborazo, and I've wandered
    in Peru ;

I've camped on Kinchinjunga, and I've crossed
    the Great Karoo.

I've drifted on the Hoang-ho, the Nile and
    Amazon ;

I've swam the Tiber and the Po " . . . thus I was
    going on,

When Jobson yawned above his beer, and
    rumbled : " Is that so. . . .
It's been so damned exciting here, too bad you
    had to go.
We've had the devil of a slump ; the market's
    gone to pot ;
You should have stuck around, you chump,
    you've missed an awful lot."

    .   .   .   .   .

In haggard lands where ages brood, on plains
    burnt out and dim,
I broke the bread of brotherhood with ruthless
    men and grim.
By ways untrod I walked with God, by parched
    and bitter path ;
In deserts dim I talked with Him, and learned to
    know His Wrath.
But in a pub that's off the Strand, sits Jobson
    every night,
And tells me what a fool I am, and maybe he is
    right.
For Jobson is a man of stamp, and proud of him
    am I ;
And I am just a bloody tramp, and will be till I
    die.

BASTARD

THE very skies were black with shame,
As near my moment drew ;
The very hour before you came
I felt I hated you.

But now I see how fair you are,
How deep divine your eyes,
It seems I step upon a star
And leap to Paradise.

What care I who your father was :
('Twere better not to know) ;
You're mine and mine alone because
I love and love you so.

What though you only bear my name,
I hold my head on high ;
For none shall have a right to claim
A right to you but I.

Because I've borne a human life,
I'm worthier, I know,
Than those who flaunt the name of wife,
And have no seed to show.

I have fulfilled, I think with joy,
My woman's destiny ;
And glad am I you are a boy,
For you will fight for me.

And maybe there will come a day
You'll bear a famous name,
And men will be ashamed to say :
" He was a child of shame."

A day will dawn, divinely free,
With love in every breast,
When every child will welcome be,
And every mother blest.

When every woman, wed or no,
Will deem her highest good
On grateful mankind to bestow
The Gift of Motherhood.

I

BESSIE'S BOIL

A LANCASHIRE BALLAD

Says I to my Missis : " Ba goom, lass ! you've
    something, I see, on your mind."
Says she : " You are right, Sam, I've something.
    It 'appens it's on me be'ind.
A Boil as 'ud make Job be jealous. It 'urts me no
    end when I sit."
Says I : " Go to 'ospittel, Missis. They might
    'ave to coot it a bit."
Says she : " I just 'ate to be showin' the part of
    me person it's at."
Says I : " Don't be fussy ; them doctors sees
    sights far more 'orrid than that."

So Missis goes off togged up tasty, and there at
    the 'ospittel door
They tells 'er to see the 'ouse Doctor, 'oose office
    is Room Thirty-four.

So she 'unts up and down till she finds it, and
    knocks and a voice says : " Come in,"
And there is a 'andsome young feller, in white
    from 'is 'eels to 'is chin.
" I've got a big boil," says my Missis. " It 'urts
    me for fair when I sit,
And Sam (that's me 'usband) 'as asked me to ask
    you to coot it a bit."
Then blushin' she plucks up her courage, and
    bravely she shows 'im the place,
And 'e gives it a proper inspection, wi' a 'eap o'
    surprise on 'is face.
Then 'e says wi' an accent o' Scotland : " Whit
    ye hae is a bile, Ah can feel,
But ye'd better consult the heid Dockter ; they
    caw him Professor O'Neil.
He's special for biles and carbuncles. Ye'll find
    him in Room Sixty-three.
No charge, Ma'am. It's been a rale pleasure.
    Jist tell him ye're comin' from me."

So Missis she thanks 'im politely, and 'unts up
    and down as before,
Till she comes to a big 'andsome room with
    " Professor O'Neil " on the door.

Then once more she plucks up her courage, and
    knocks, and a voice says : "All right."
So she enters, and sees a fat feller wi' whiskers,
    all togged up in white.
"I've got a big boil," says my Missis, "And if ye
    will kindly permit,
I'd like for to 'ave you inspect it ; it 'urts me like
    all when I sit."
So blushin' as red as a beet-root she 'astens to
    show 'im the spot,
And 'e says wi' a look o' amazement : "Sure,
    Ma'am, it must hurrt ye a lot."
Then 'e puts on 'is specs to regard it, and finally
    says wi' a frown :
"I'll bet it's as sore as the divvle, espacially whin
    ye sit down.
I think it's a case for the Surgeon ; ye'd better
    consult Doctor Hoyle.
I've no hisitation in sayin' yer boil is a hill of a
    boil."

So Missis she thanks 'im for sayin' her boil is a
    hill of a boil,
And 'unts all around till she comes on a door that
    is marked : "Doctor Hoyle."

But by now she 'as fair got the wind up, and
    trembles in every limb ;

But she thinks : " After all, 'e's a Doctor. Ah
    moosn't be baashful wi' 'im."

She's made o' good stoof is the Missis, so she
    knocks and a voice says : " 'Oos there ? "

" It's me," says ma Bessie, an' enters a room
    which is spacious and bare.

And a wise-lookin' old feller greets 'er, and 'e too
    is togged up in white.

" It's the room where they coot ye," thinks
    Bessie ; and shakes like a jelly wi'
    fright.

" Ah got a big boil," begins Missis, " And if ye
    are sure you don't mind,

I'd like ye to see it a moment. It 'urts me,
    because it's be'ind."

So thinkin' she'd best get it over, she 'astens to
    show 'im the place,

And 'e stares at 'er kindo surprised like, an' gets
    very red in the face.

But 'e looks at it most conscientious, from every
    angle of view,

Then 'e says wi' a shrug o' 'is shoulders : " Pore
    Lydy, I'm sorry for you.

It wants to be cut, but you should 'ave a medical
    bloke to do that.
Sye, why don't yer go to the *'orsespittel*, where all
    the *Doctors* is at ?
Ye see, Ma'am, this part o' the buildin' is closed
    on account o' repairs ;
Us fellers is only the pynters, a-pyntin' the 'alls
    and the stairs."

FIVE-PER-CENT

BECAUSE I have ten thousand pounds I sit upon
    my stern,
And leave my living tranquilly for other folks to
    earn.
For in some procreative way that isn't very clear,
Ten thousand pounds will breed, they say, five
    hundred every year.
So as I have a healthy hate of economic strife,
I mean to stand aloof from it the balance of my
    life.
And yet with sympathy I see the grimy son of
    toil,
And heartily congratulate the tiller of the soil.
I like the miner in the mine, the sailor on the sea,
Because up to five hundred pounds they sail and
    mine for me.
For me their toil is taxed unto that annual extent,
According to the holy shibboleth of Five-per-
    Cent.

So get ten thousand pounds, my friend, in any
    way you can,
And leave your future welfare to the noble
    Working Man.
He'll buy you suits of Harris tweed, an Airedale
    and a car ;
Your golf clubs and your morning *Times*, your
    whisky and cigar.
He'll cosily install you in a cottage by a stream,
With every modern comfort, and a garden that's
    a dream.
Or if your tastes be urban, he'll provide you with
    a flat,
Secluded from the clamour of the proletariat.
With pictures, music, easy chairs, a table of good
    cheer,
A chap can manage nicely on five hundred pounds
    a year.
And though around you painful signs of industry
    you view,
Why should you work when you can make your
    money work for you.

So I'll get down upon my knees and bless the
    Working Man,

Who offers me a life of ease through all my
    mortal span ;
Whose loins are lean to make me fat, who slaves
    to keep me free,
Who dies before his prime to let me round the
    century ;
Whose wife and children toil in turn until their
    strength is spent,
That I may live in idleness upon my five-per-
    cent.
And if at times they curse me, why should I feel
    any blame ?
For in my place I know that they would do the
    very same.
Aye, though they hoist a flag that's red on Sunday
    afternoon,
Just offer them ten thousand pounds and see
    them change their tune.
So I'll enjoy my dividends and live my life with
    zest,
And bless the mighty men who first—*invented
    Interest.*

SECURITY

THERE once was a limpet puffed with pride
Who said to the ribald sea :
" It isn't I who cling to the rock,
It's the rock who clings to me ;
It's the silly old rock who hugs me tight,
Because he loves me so ;
And though I struggle with all my might,
He will not let me go.

Then said the sea, who hates the rock
That defies him night and day :
" You want to be free —well, leave it to me,
I'll help you to get away.
I know such a beautiful silver beach,
Where blissfully you may bide ;
Shove off to-night when the moon is bright,
And I'll swing you there on my tide."

" I'd like to go," said the limpet low,

" But what's a silver beach ? "
" It's sand," said the sea, " bright baby rocks,
And you shall be lord of each."
" Righto ! " said the limpet ; " Life allures,
And a rover I would be."
So greatly bold she slacked her hold
And launched on the laughing sea.

But when she got to the gelid deep
Where the waters swish and swing,
She began to know with a sense of woe
That a limpet's lot is to cling.
But she couldn't cling to a jelly fish,
Or clutch at a wastrel weed,
So she raised a cry as the waves went by,
But the waves refused to heed.

Then when she came to the glaucous deep
Where the congers coil and leer,
The flesh in her shell began to creep,
And she shrank in utter fear.
It was good to reach that silver beach,
That gleamed in the morning light,
Where a shining band of the silver sand
Looked up with a welcome bright.

Looked up with a smile that was full of guile,
Called up through the crystal blue :
" Each one of us is a baby rock,
And we want to cling to you."
Then the heart of the limpet leaped with joy,
For she hated the waters wide ;
So down she sank to the sandy bank
That clung to her under-side.

That clung so close she couldn't breathe,
So fierce she fought to be free ;
But the silver sand couldn't understand,
While above her laughed the sea.
Then to each wave that wimpled past
She cried in her woe and pain :
" Oh take me back, let me rivet fast
To my steadfast rock again."

She cried till she roused a taxi-crab
Who gladly gave her a ride ;
But I grieve to say in his crabby way
He insisted she sit inside. . . .
So if of the limpet breed ye be,
Beware life's brutal shock ;
Don't take the chance of the changing sea,
But—*cling like hell to your rock.*

LONGEVITY

I WATCHED one day a parrot grey—'twas in a
    barber shop.
" Cuckold ! " he cried, until I sighed : " You
    feathered devil, stop ! "
Then balefully he looked at me, and slid along
    his perch,
With sneering eye that seemed to pry my very
    soul to search.
So fierce, so bold, so grim, so cold, so *agate* was
    his stare :
And then that bird I thought I heard this senti-
    ment declare :—

" As it appears, a hundred years a parrot may
    survive,
When you are gone I'll sit upon this perch and be
    alive.
In this same spot I'll drop my crot, and crack my
    sunflower seeds,

And cackle loud when in a shroud you rot be-
      neath the weeds.
I'll carry on when carrion you lie beneath the
      yew ;
With claw and beak my grub I'll seek when grubs
      are seeking you."

" Foul fowl ! " said I, " Don't prophesy.   I'll
      jolly well contrive
That when I rot in bone-yard lot *you* cease to be
      alive."
So I bespoke that barber bloke :   " Joe, here's a
      five-pound note.
It's crisp and new, and yours if you will slice that
      parrot's throat."
" In part," says he, " I must agree, for poor I be
      in pelf.
With right good will I'll take your bill, but—cut
      his throat yourself."

So it occurred I took that bird to my ancestral
      hall,
And there he sat and sniggered at the portraits on
      the wall.

I sought to cut his wind-pipe but he gave me such
 a peck,

So cross was I, I swore I'd try to wring his
 blasted neck ;

When shrill he cried : " It's *parrotcide* what you
 propose to do ;

For every time you make a rhyme you're just a
 parrot too."

Said I : " It's true. I bow to you. Poor parrots
 are we all."

And now I sense with reverence the wisdom in
 his poll.

For every time I want a rhyme he seems to find
 the word ;

In any doubt he helps me out—a most amazing
 bird.

This line that lies before your eyes he helped me
 to indite ;

I sling the ink but often think it's he who ought
 to write.

It's he who should in mystic mood concoct
 poetic screeds,

And I who ought to drop my crot and crackle
 sunflower seeds.

A parrot nears a hundred years (or so the legend
    goes),
So were I he this century I might see to its
    close.
Then I might swing within my ring while revolu-
    tions roar,
And watch a world to ruin hurled—and find it all
    a bore.
As upside-down I cling and clown, I might with
    parrot eyes
Blink blandly when exalted men are moulding
    Paradise.
New Christs might die, while grimly I would
    croak and carry on,
Till gnarled and old I should behold the year
    TWO THOUSAND dawn.

But what a fate ! How I should hate upon my
    perch to sit,
And nothing do to make anew a world for angels
    fit.
No, better far, though feeble are my lyric notes
    and flat,
Be dead and done than anyone who lives a life
    like that.

Though critic-scarred a humble bard I feel I'd
    rather be,
Than flap and flit and shriek and spit through all
    a century.

So, feathered friend, until the end you may divide
    my den,
And make a mess, which (more or less) I clean up
    now and then.
But I prefer the doom to share of dead and gone
    compeers,
Than parrot be, and live to see *ten times* a hundred
    years.

K

RESIGNATION

I'D hate to be a centipede (of legs I've only two),
For if new trousers I should need (as oftentimes
    I do),
The bill would come to such a lot 'twould tax an
    Astorbilt,
Or else I'd have to turn a Scot and caper in a kilt.

I'm jolly glad I haven't got a neck like a giraffe.
I'd want to tie it in a knot and shorten it by half.
Or, as I wear my collars high, how laundry men
    would gloat !
And what a lot of beer I'd buy to lubricate my
    throat !

I'd hate to be a goldfish, snooping round a
    crystal globe,
A naughty little bold fish, that disdains chemise
    or robe.

The public stare I couldn't bear, if naked as a
    stone,
And when my toilet I prepare, I'd rather be alone.

I'd hate to be an animal, an insect or a fish.
To be the least like bird or beast I've not the
    slightest wish.
It's best, I find, to be resigned, and stick to
    Nature's plan :
Content am I to live and die, just—Ordinary
    MAN.

PRIVACY

Oh you who are shy of the popular eye,
(Though most of us seek to survive it),
Just think of the goldfish who wanted to die
Because she could never be private.
There are pebbles and reeds for aquarium needs
Of eel and of pike who are bold fish ;
But who gives a thought to a sheltering spot
For the sensitive soul of a goldfish ?

So the poor little thing swam round in a ring,
In a globe of a crystalline crudity ;
Swam round and swam round, but no refuge she
    found
From the public display of her nudity ;
No weedy retreat for a cloister discreet,
From the eye of the mob to exempt her ;
Can you wonder she paled, and her appetite
    failed,
Till even a fly couldn't tempt her ?

I watched with dismay as she faded away ;
Each day she grew slimmer and slimmer.
From an amber that burned, to a silver she
    turned
Then swiftly was dimmer and dimmer.
No longer she gleamed, like a spectre she seemed,
One morning I anxiously sought her :
I only could stare—she no longer was there . . .
She'd simply dissolved in the water.

So when you behold bright fishes of gold,
In globes of immaculate purity ;
Just think how they'd be more contented and
    free
If you gave them a little obscurity.
And you who make laws, get busy because
You can brighten the lives of untold fish,
If its sadness you note, and a measure promote
To Ensure Private Life For The Goldfish.

MATERNITY

THERE once was a Square, such a square little
    Square,
And he loved a trim Triangle ;
But she was a flirt and around her skirt
Vainly she made him dangle.
Oh he wanted to wed and he had no dread
Of domestic woes and wrangles ;
For he thought that his fate was to procreate
Cute little Squares and Triangles.

Now it happened one day on that geometric way
There swaggered a big bold Cube,
With a haughty stare and he made that Square
Have the air of a perfect boob ;
To his solid spell the Triangle fell,
And she thrilled with love's sweet sickness,
For she took delight in his breadth and height—
But how she adored his thickness !

So that poor little Square just died of despair,
For his love he could not strangle ;
While the bold Cube led to the bridal bed
That cute and acute Triangle.
The Square's sad lot she has long forgot,
And his passionate pretensions . . .
For she dotes on her kids—Oh such cute
 Pyramids
In a world of three dimensions.

VIRGINITY

My mother she had children five and four are
  dead and gone ;
While I, least worthy to survive, persist in living
  on.
She looks at me, I must confess, sometimes with
  spite and bitterness.

My mother is three-score and ten, while I am
  forty-three.
You don't know how it hurts me when we go
  somewhere to tea,
And people tell her on the sly we look like sisters,
  she and I.

It hurts to see her secret glee ; but most, because
  it's true.
Sometimes I think she thinks that she looks
  younger of the two.

Oh as I gently take her arm, how I would love
    to do her harm !

For ever since I came from school she put it in
    my head
I was a weakling and a fool, a " born old maid "
    she said.
" You'll always stay at home," sighed she, " and
    keep your Mother company."

Oh pity is a bitter brew ; I've drunk it to the
    lees ;
For there is little else to do but do my best to
    please :
My life has been so little worth I curse the hour
    she gave me birth.

I curse the hour she gave me breath, who never
    wished me wife ;
My happiest day will be the death of her who
    gave me life ;
I hate her for the life she gave : I hope to dance
    upon her grave.

She's wearing roses in her hat ; I wince to hear
    her say :

" Poor Alice this, poor Alice that," she drains my
    joy away.
It seems to brace her up that she can pity, pity,
    pity me.

You'll see us walking in the street, with careful
    step and slow ;
And people often say : " How sweet ! " as arm in
    arm we go.
Like chums we never are apart—yet oh the
    hatred in my heart !

My chest is weak, and I might be (O God !) the
    first to go.
For her what triumph that would be—she thinks
    of it, I know.
To outlive all her kith and kin—how she would
    glow beneath her skin !

She says she will not make her Will, until she
    takes to bed ;
She little thinks if thoughts could kill, to-morrow
    she'd be dead. . . .
" *Please come to breakfast, Mother dear ; Your
    coffee will be cold, I fear.*"

SENSIBILITY

I

ONCE, when a boy, *I killed a cat*.
I guess it's just because of that
A cat evokes my tenderness,
And takes so kindly my caress.
For with a rich, resonant purr
It sleeks an arch of ardent fur
So vibrantly against my shin ;
And as I tickle tilted chin
And rub the roots of velvet ears
Its tail in undulation rears.
Then tremoring with all its might,
In blissful sensuous delight,
It looks aloft with lambent eyes,
Mystic, Egyptianly wise,
And O so eloquently tries
In every fibre to express
Consummate trust and friendliness.

II

I think the longer that we live
The more do we grow sensitive
Of hurt and harm to man and beast,
And learn to suffer at the least
Surmise of other's suffering ;
Till pity, like an eager spring
Wells up, and we are over-fain
To vibrate to the chords of pain.

For look you—after three-score years
I see with anguish nigh to tears
That starveling cat so sudden still
I set my terrier to kill.
Great, golden memories pale away,
But that unto my dying day
Will haunt and haunt me horribly.
Why, even my poor dog felt shame
And shrank away as if the blame
Of that poor mangled mother-cat
Would ever lie at *his* doormat.

III

What's done is done.   No power can bring

To living joy a slaughtered thing.
Aye, if of life I gave my own
I could not for my guilt atone.
And though in stress of sea and land
Sweet breath has ended at my hand,
That boyhood killing in my eyes
A thousand must epitomize.

Yet to my twilight steals a thought :
Somehow forgiveness may be bought ;
Somewhere I'll live my life again
So finely sensitized to pain,
With heart so rhymed to ruth and right
That Truth will be a blaze of light ;
And all the evil I have wrought
Will haggardly to home be brought. . . .
Then will I know my hell indeed,
And bleed where I made others bleed,
Till purged by penitence of sin
To Peace (or Heaven) I may win.

Well, anyway, you know the why
We are so pally, cats and I ;
So if you have the gift of shame,
O Fellow-sinner, be the same.

INFIDELITY

Three Triangles

TRIANGLE ONE

My husband put some poison in my beer,
And fondly hoped that I would drink it up.
He would get rid of me—no bloody fear,
For when his back was turned I changed the cup.
He took it all, and if he did not die,
It's just because he's heartier than I.

And now I watch and watch him night and day
Dreading that he will try it on again.
I'm getting like a skeleton they say,
And every time I feel the slightest pain
I think : he's got me this time. . . . Oh the beast!
He might have let me starve to death, at least.

But all he thinks of is that shell-pink nurse.
I know as well as well that they're in love.

I'm sure they kiss, and maybe do things worse,
Although she looks as gentle as a dove.
I see their eyes with passion all aglow :
I know they only wait for me to go.

Ah well, I'll go (I have to, anyway),
But they will pay the price of lust and sin.
I've sent a letter to the police to say :
" If I should die it's them have done me in."
And now a lot of veronal I'll take,
And go to sleep, and never, never wake.

*But won't I laugh ! Aye, even when I'm dead,
To think of them both hanging by the head.*

TRIANGLE TWO

My wife's a fancy bit of stuff, it's true ;
But that's no reason she should do me dirt.
Of course I know a girl is tempted to,
With mountain men a-fussin' round her skirt.
A 'andsome woman's bound to 'ave a 'eart,
But that's no reason she should be a tart.

I didn't oughter give me 'ome address
To sergeant when 'e last went on 'is leave ;
And now the 'ole shebang's a bloody mess ;
I didn't think the missis would deceive.
And 'ere was I, a-riskin' of me life,
And there was 'e, a-sleepin' wiv me wife.

Go' blimy, but this thing 'as got to stop.
Well, next time when we makes a big attack,
As soon as we gets well across the top,
I'll plug 'im (accidental) in the back.
'E'll cop a blinkin' packet in 'is spine,
And that'll be the end of 'im, the swine.

It's easy in the muck-up of a fight ;
And all me mates'll think it was the foe.
And 'oo can say it doesn't serve 'im right ?
And I'll go 'ome, and none will ever know.
My missis didn't oughter do that sort o' thing,
Seein' as 'ow she wears my weddin' ring.

Well, we'll be just as 'appy as before,
When otherwise she might a' bin a 'ore.

TRIANGLE THREE

It's fun to see Joe fuss around that kid.
I know 'e loves 'er more than all the rest,
Because she's by a lot the prettiest.
'E wouldn't lose 'er for a 'undred quid.
I love 'er too, because she isn't his'n ;
But Jim, his brother's, wot they've put in prison.

It's 'ard to 'ave a 'usband wot you 'ate ;
So soft that if 'e knowed you'd 'ad a tup,
'E wouldn't 'ave the guts to beat you up.
Now Jim—'e's wot I call a proper mate.
I daren't try no monkey tricks wiv 'im.
'E'd flay me 'ide off (quite right, too) would Jim.

I won't let on to Jim when 'e comes out ;
But Joe—each time I see 'im kissin' Nell,
I 'ave to leave the room and laugh like 'ell.
'E'll 'ave the benefit (damn little) of the doubt.
So let 'im kiss our Nellie fit to smother ;
There aint no *proof* 'er father is 'is brother.

Well, anyway I've no remorse. You see,
I've kept my frailty in the family.

L

LAUGHTER

I LAUGH at Life : its antics make for me a giddy
    game,
Where only foolish fellows take themselves with
    solemn aim.
I laugh at pomp and vanity, at riches, rank and
    pride ;
At social inanity, at swagger, swank and side.
At poets, pastry-cooks and kings, at folk sublime
    and small,
Who fuss about a thousand things that matter
    not at all ;
At those who dream of name and fame, at those
    who scheme for pelf. . . .
But best of all the laughing game—is laughing at
    myself.

Some poet chap has labelled man the noblest
    work of God :
I see myself a charlatan, a humbug and a fraud.
Yea, 'spite of show and shallow wit, and senti-
    mental drool,

I know myself a hypocrite, a coward and a fool.

And though I kick myself with glee profoundly
on the pants,

I'm little worse, it seems to me, than other
human ants.

For if you probe your private mind, impervious
to shame,

Oh, Gentle Reader, you may find you're much
about the same.

Then let us mock with ancient mirth this comic,
cosmic plan ;

The stars are laughing at the earth ; God's
greatest joke is man.

For laughter is a buckler bright, and scorn a
shining spear ;

So let us laugh with all our might at folly, fraud
and fear.

Yet on our sorry selves be spent our most sar-
donic glee.

Oh don't pay Life the compliment to take it *seriously*.

For he who can himself despise, be surgeon to
the bone,

May win to worth in other's eyes, to wisdom
in his own.

LAZINESS

Let laureates sing with a rapturous swing
Of the wonder and glory of work ;
Let pulpiteers preach and with passion impeach
The indolent wretches who shirk.
No doubt they are right : in the stress of the
  fight
It's the slackers who go to the wall ;
So though it's my shame I perversely proclaim
It's fine to do nothing at all.

It's fine to recline on the flat of one's spine,
With never a thought in one's head :
It's lovely to lie staring up at the sky
When others are earning their bread.
It's great to feel one with the soil and the sun,
Drowned deep in the grasses so tall ;
Oh it's noble to sweat, pounds and dollars to get,
But—it's grand to do nothing at all.

So sing to the praise of the fellows who laze
Instead of lambasting the soil ;
The vagabonds gay who lounge by the way,
Conscientious objectors to toil.
But lest you should think, by this spatter of ink,
The Muses still hold me in thrall,
I'll round off my rhyme, and (until the next
    time)
Work like hell—doing nothing at all.

ACCORDIAN

Some carol of the banjo, to its measure keeping
    time ;
Of viol or of lute some make a song.
My battered old accordian, you're worthy of a
    rhyme,
You've been my friend and comforter so long.
Round half the world I've trotted you, a dozen
    years or more ;
You've given heaps of people lots of fun ;
You've set a host of happy feet a-tapping on the
    floor . . .
Alas ! your dancing days are nearly done.

I've played you from the palm-belt to the suburbs
    of the Pole ;
From the silver-tipped sierras to the sea.
The gay and gilded cabin and the grimy glory-
    hole
Have echoed to your impish melody.

I've hushed you in the dug-out when the trench
    was stiff with dead ;
I've lulled you by the coral-laced lagoon ;
I've packed you on a camel from the dung-fire on
    the *bled*,
To the hell-for-breakfast Mountains of the
    Moon.

I've ground you to the shanty men, a-whooping
    heel and toe,
And the hula-hula graces in the glade.
I've swung you in the igloo to the lousy Esquimo,
And the Haussa at a hundred in the shade.
The nigger on the *levee*, and the Dinka by the
    Nile
Have shuffled to your insolent appeal.
I've rocked with glee the chimpanzee, and
    mocked the crocodile,
And shocked the pompous penguin and the seal.

I've set the yokels singing in a little Surrey pub,
Apaches swinging in a Belville bar.
I've played an obbligato to the tom-tom's rub-a-
    dub,
And the throb of Andalusian guitar.

From the Horn to Honolulu, from the Cape to
    Kalmazoo,
From Wick to Wicklow, Samarkand to Spain,
You've roughed it with my kit-bag like a comrade
    tried and true. . . .
Old pal ! We'll never hit the trail again.

Oh I know you're cheap and vulgar, you're an
    instrumental crime.
In drawing-rooms you haven't got a show.
You're a musical abortion, you're the voice of
    grit and grime,
You're the spokesman of the lowly and the low.
You're a democratic devil, you're the darling of
    the mob ;
You're a wheezy, breezy blasted bit of glee.
You're the headache of the high-brow, you're the
    horror of the snob,
But you're worth your weight in ruddy gold to
    me.

For you've chided me in weakness and you've
    cheered me in defeat ;
You've been an anodyne in hours of pain ;

And when the slugging jolts of life have jarred me
    off my feet,
You've ragged me back into the ring again.
I'll never go to Heaven, for I know I am not fit,
The golden harps of harmony to swell ;
But with asbestos bellows, if the devil will permit,
I'll swing you to the fork-tailed imps of Hell.
Yes, I'll hank you, and I'll spank you,
And I'll everlasting yank you
To the cinder-swinging satellites of Hell.

TREES AGAINST THE SKY

Pines against the sky,
Pluming the purple hill ;
Pines . . . and I wonder why,
Heart, you quicken and thrill ?
Wistful heart of a boy,
Fill with a strange sweet joy,
Lifting to Heaven nigh—
Pines against the sky.

Palms against the sky,
Flailing the hot, hard blue ;
Stark on the beach I lie,
Dreaming horizons new ;
Heart of my youth elate,
Scorning a humdrum fate,
Keyed to adventure high—
Palms against the sky.

Oaks against the sky,

Ramparts of leaves high-hurled,
Staunch to stand and defy
All the winds of the world ;
Stalwart and proud and free,
Firing the man in me
To try and again to try—
Oaks against the sky.

Olives against the sky
Of evening, limpidly bright ;
Tranquil and soft and shy,
Dreaming in amber light ;
Breathing the peace of life,
Ease after toil and strife. . . .
Hark to their silver sigh !
Olives against the sky.

Cypresses glooming the sky,
Stark at the end of the road ;
Failing and faint am I,
Lief to be eased of my load ;
There where the stones peer white
In the last of the silvery light,
Quiet and cold I'll lie—
Cypresses etching the sky.

Trees, trees against the sky —
O I have loved them well !
There are pleasures you cannot buy,
Treasures you cannot sell,
And not the smallest of these
Is the gift and glory of trees. . . .
So I gaze and I know now why
It is good to live—and to die. . . .
Trees and the Infinite Sky.

MOON-LOVER

I

The Moon is like a ping-pong ball ;
I lean against the orchard wall,
And see it soar into the void,
A silky sphere of celluloid.

Then fairy fire enkindles it,
Like gossamer by taper lit,
Until it glows above the trees
As mellow as a Cheddar cheese.

And up and up I watch it press
Into appalling loneliness ;
Like realms of ice without a stain,
A corpse Moon come to life again.

Ruthless it drowns a sturdy star
That seeks its regal way to bar ;
Seeming with conscious power to grow,
And sweeter, purer, gladder glow.

Dreaming serenely up the sky,
Until exultantly on high,
It shimmers with superb delight,
The silver navel of the night.

II

I HAVE a compact to commune
A monthly midnight with the Moon ;
Into its face I stare and stare,
And find sweet understanding there.

As quiet as a toad I sit
And tell my tale of days to it ;
The tessellated yarn I've spun
In thirty spells of star and sun.

And the Moon listens pensively,
As placid as a lamb to me ;
Until I think there's just us two
In silver world of mist and dew.

In all of spangled space, but I
To stare moon-struck into the sky ;

Of billion being I alone
To praise the Moon as still as stone,

And seal a bond between us two,
Closer than mortal ever knew ;
For as mute masses I intone
The Moon is mine and mine alone.

III

To know the Moon as few men may,
One must be just a little *fey* ;
And for our friendship's sake I'm glad
That I am just a trifle mad,

And one with all the wild, wise things,
The furtive folk of fur and wings,
That hold the Moon within their eyes,
And make it nightly sacrifice.

O I will watch the maiden Moon
Dance on the sea with silver shoon ;
But with the Queen Moon I will keep
My tryst when all the world's asleep.

As I have kept by land and sea
That tryst for half a century ;
Entranced in sibylline suspense
Beyond a world of common-sense.

Until one night the Moon alone
Will look upon a graven stone. . . .
I wonder will it miss me then,
Its lover more than other men ?

Or will my wistful ghost be there,
Down ages dim to stare and stare,
On silver nights without a stir—
The Moon's Eternal Worshipper ?

LITTLE PUDDLETON

I

*Let others sing of Empire and of pomp beyond the
    sea,*
A song of Little Puddleton is good enough for me,
*A song of kindly living, and of coming home to
    tea.*

I SELDOM read the papers, so I don't know what
    goes on.
I go to bed at sunset, and I leap alert at dawn,
To gossip with my garden, which I'll have you
    understand,
Is the neatest and the sweetest little garden in the
    land ;
A span of sunny quietude, with walls so high and
    stout,
They shut me in from all the world, and shut the
    whole world out,
So that its sad bewilderment seems less than true
    to me :

As placid as a pool I live, as tranquil as a tree ;
And all its glory I would give for glint of linnet's
  wings ;
My cabbages are more to me than continents and
  kings.
Dominion have I of my own, where feud and
  faction cease,
A heaven of tranquillity, a paradise of peace.

II

*Let continents be bathed in blood and cities leap
  in flame ;*
*The life of Little Puddleton goes on and on the
  same ;*
Its ritual we follow, as we play a pleasant game.

THE village worthies sit and smoke their long-
  stemmed pipes of clay,
And cheerily they nod to me, and pass the time
  of day.
We talk of pigs and clover, and the prospect of
  the crops,
And the price of eggs and butter—there the con-
  versation drops.

For in a doubt-distracted world I keep the rustic
    touch :
I think it's better not to think too deeply nor too
    much ;
But just to dream and take delight in all I hear
    and see,
The tinker in the tavern, with his trollop on his
    knee ;
The ivied church, the anvil clang, the geese upon
    the green,
The drowsy noon, the hush of eve so holy and
    serene.
This is my world, then back again with heart of
    joy I go
To cottage walls of mellow stain, and garden all
    aglow.

III

For all I've been and all I've seen I have no vain
    regret.
One comes to Little Puddleton, contented to forget;
Accepting village values, immemorially set.

I DID not make this world and so it's not my job
    to mend ;
But I have fought for fifty years and now I near
    the end ;
And I am heart-faint from the fight, and claim
    the right to rest,
And dare to hope the last of life will prove to be
    the best.
For here have I four sturdy walls with low and
    humble thatch,
A smiling little orchard and a big potato patch.
And so with hoe in hand I stand and mock the
    dubious sky ;
Let revolution rock the land, serene, secure am I.
I grow my simple food, I groom my lettuce and
    my beans ;
I feast in colour, form and song, and ask not what
    it means.
Beauty suffices in itself ; then when my strength
    is spent,
Like simple hind with empty mind, I cultivate
    content.

Behold then Little Puddleton, the end of all my
    dreams.

Not much to show for life, I know ; yet O how
        sweet it seems !
For when defeated day goes down in carnage in
        the West,
How blessed sanctuary is, and peace and love and
        rest !

BOOKSHELF

I LIKE to think that when I fall,
A rain-drop in Death's shoreless sea,
This shelf of books along the wall,
Beside my bed, will mourn for me.

Regard it. . . . Aye, my taste is queer.
Some of my bards you may disdain.
Shakespeare and Milton are not here ;
Shelley and Keats you seek in vain.
Wordsworth, Tennyson, Browning too,
Remarkably are not in view.

Who are they ? *Omar* first you see,
With Vine and Rose and Nightingale,
Voicing my pet philosophy
Of Wine and Song. . . .Then *Reading Gaol*,
Where Fate a gruesome pattern makes,
And dawn-light shudders as it wakes.

The *Ancient Mariner* is next,
With eerie and terrific text ;
Then Burns, with pawky human touch —
Poor devil ! I have loved him much.
And now a gay quartette behold :
Bret Harte and Eugene Field are here ;
And Henley, chanting brave and bold,
And Chesterton, in praise of Beer.

Lastly come valiant Singers three ;
To whom this strident Day belongs :
Kipling, to whom I bow the knee,
Masefield, with rugged sailor songs. . . .
And to my lyric troupe I add
With grateful heart—*The Shropshire Lad.*

Behold my minstrels, just eleven.
For half my life I've loved them well.
And though I have no hope of Heaven,
And more than Highland fear of Hell,
May I be damned if on this shelf
Ye find a rhyme I make myself.

FIVE FRIVOLOUS SONGS

You Can't Can Love
Lip-stick Liz
The Bread-knife Ballad
The Boola-boola Maid
The Song of a Sardine

[These are included in *Bath-Tub Ballads*, with Music by the author, and published by Messrs. Francis, Day & Hunter, London.]

YOU CAN'T CAN LOVE

Oʜ I don't know how fishes feel,
But I can't help thinking it odd
That a gay young flapper of a female Eel
Should fall in love with a Cod.
Yet that's exactly what she did,
And it only goes to prove
That whatever you do you can't put the lid
On that crazy feeling, Love. (*Chorus*.)

   . . . .

Now that young Tom Cod was a dreadful rake
And he had no wish to wed ;
But he feared that the poor thing's heart would
  break,
So this is what he said :
" Some fellows prize a woman's eyes,
And some admire her lips ;
While some have a taste for a tiny waist,
But me, what I like is—ʜɪᴘs." (*Chorus*.)

   . . . .

187

" So you see, my dear," said the gay Tom Cod,
" Exactly how I feel.
Oh I hate to be unkind, but I know my mind,
And there ain't no hips on an eel."
" Alas ! it's true," said the foolish fish
As she blushed to her finny tips ;
" And with might and main, though it gives me
     pain,
I'll try to develop HIPS." (*Chorus.*)

. . . . .

So day and night with all her might
She physical culturized ;
But alas and alack! in the middle of her back
No hump she recognized.
And then she knew her love's eclipse
Was fated from the start ;
For you never yet saw an eel with HIPS,
So she died of a broken heart. (*Chorus.*)

Chorus after each verse :—
Oh you gotta hand it out to Love, to Love,
You can't can Love ;
You'll find it at the bottom of the briny deep
And the blue above.
From the Belgian Hare to the Polar Bear

And the Turtle Dove,
You can look where you please, but from
    elephants to fleas . . .

Verse 2 :

You can look where you like, but from pollywogs
    to pike . . .

Verse 3 :

You can look where you choose, but from crabs
    to kangaroos . . .

Verse 4 :

You can look where you please, but from buffaloes
    to bees . . .

YOU'LL NEVER PUT THE LID ON LOVE.

LIP-STICK LIZ

OH Lip-stick Liz was in the biz'
That's the oldest known in history ;
She had a lot of fancy rags,
Of her form she made no mystery.
She had a man, a fancy man,
His name was Alexander ;
And he used to beat her up because
He couldn't understand her.

  . . . . .

Now Lip-stick Liz she loved her man,
And she couldn't love no other ;
So when she saw him with a Broadway blonde
Her rage she could not smother.
Oh she saw them once and she saw them twice,
But the third time nearly crazed her ;
So she walked into a hardware store
And she bought a brand-new razor.

  . . . . .

Now Lip-stick Liz she trailed them two,
For she was tired of weeping ;
She trailed them two to a flash hotel,
And there she found them sleeping.
So she gashed them once and she gashed them
    twice,
Their jug'lar veins to sever ;
And the bright blood flowed in a pool between,
And their lives were done forever.

. . . . .

Now Lip-stick Liz she went to the police
And says she : " Me hands are gory ;
And ye'll put me away in a deep dark cell
When once you've heard me story."
So they've put her away in a deep dark cell
Until her life be over :
And what is the moral of the whole damn show
I wish I could discover.

    Chorus after each verse :—
    Oh Lip-stick Liz !
    What a lousy life this is !
    It's a hell of a break
    For a girl on the make—
    Oh Lip-stick Liz !

BREAD-KNIFE BALLAD

I

A LITTLE child was sitting
Upon her mother's knee,
And down her cheeks the bitter tears did flow ;
And as I sadly listened
I heard this tender plea ;
'Twas uttered in a voice so soft and low :—

Chorus :

Please, Mother, don't stab Father with the
    Bread-knife.
Remember 'twas a gift when you were wed.
But if you *must* stab Father with the Bread-knife,
Please, Mother, use another for the bread.

II

" Not guilty ! " said the Jury,
And the Judge said : " Set her free ;
But remember, it must not occur again ;

And next time you must listen
To your little daughter's plea,"
Then all the Court did join in this refrain :—
Chorus . . .

N

THE BOOLA-BOOLA MAID

In the wilds of Madagascar dwelt a Boola-boola
    Maid ;
For her hand young men would ask her, but she
    always was afraid.
Oh that Boola-boola Maid she was living in the
    shade
Of a spreading Yum-yum tree ;
And when the day was done, at the setting of the
    sun
She would sing this melody :—

Chorus :

I don't want no cave-man to caress me ;
I don't want no coal-black hands to press me.
All I want is a fellow who wears suspenders ;
That'll be the coon to whom this babe surrenders.
For the man I wed must have a proper *trousseau* :
None of your fig-leaf dudes will make me do so ;

For it's funny how I feel, but I'm crazy for Socks
    Appeal,
And my dream is to marry a man with a pair of
    socks.

While this ditty she was cooing, came a Boola-
    boola Man,
And he lost no time in wooing, for he punched
    her on the pan.
Oh that Boola-boola Maid she was terribly
    afraid,
So he punched her on the eye ;
And a woeful Maid was she, as beneath that
    Yum-yum tree
He heard that maiden cry :—

Chorus as before.

Then with shrieks of ribald laughter, said that
    Boola-boola Man :
" If it's only socks you're after, I will do the best
    I can.
Oh I've handed you a pair, and I've plenty more
    to spare,"
So he socked her on the nose ;

And then he laughed with glee as beneath that
     Yum-yum tree
This lamentation rose :

        Chorus once again.

Now the wedding tom-tom's over for this Boola-
     boola Maid,
And when evening shadows hover, she no longer
     is afraid.
For she wears a fig-leaf pinny and she rocks a
     pickininny
In the shade of the Yum-yum tree ;
And she's happy with her He Man though she
     still dreams of a She Man,
As she sings this song with glee :

        Chorus, final.

THE SONG OF A SARDINE

A FAT man sat in an orchestra stall, and his
cheeks were wet with tears,
As he gazed at the prima-donna tall whom he
hadn't seen for years.
"Oh don't you remember," he murmurs low,
"that Spring in Montparnasse,
When hand in hand we used to go to our nightly
singing class.
Ah me! those days so gay and glad, so full of
hope and cheer,
And the farewell supper that we had of tinned
sardines and beer;
When you looked so like a little Queen, with your
proud and haughty air,
That I took from the box the last sardine, and I
twined it in your hair." (*Chorus*.)

Verse two.

Alas! I am only a stock-broker now, while you
are high and great;

The laurels of Fame adorn your brow, while on
you princes wait.

And as I sit so sadly here, and list to your thrilling
tones,

You cannot remember, I sadly fear, if my name
is Smith or Jones.

Yet oh those days of long ago, when I had
scarce a *soù*!

And as my bitter tears down-flow I think again
of you.

And once again I seem to see that Maid of sweet
sixteen,

Within whose tresses tenderly I twined that
bright sardine. (*Chorus.*)

Chorus, after each verse :

Oh that sardine in your hair !
I can see it shining there,
As I took it from its box,
And I twined it in your locks.
Silver sardine in your hair
Like a jewel rich and rare—
Oh that little silver sardine in your hair !

WARSAW

I was in Warsaw when the first bomb fell ;
I was in Warsaw when the Terror came—
Havoc and horror, famine, fear and flame,
Blasting from loveliness a living hell.
Barring the station towered a sentinel ;
Trainward I battled, blind escape my aim.
ENGLAND ! I cried. He kindled at the name :
With lion-leap he haled me. . . . All was well.

ENGLAND ! they cried for aid, and cried in vain.
Vain was their valour, emptily they cried.
Bleeding, they saw their City crucified. . . .
O splendid soldier, by the last, lone train,
To-day would you flame forth to fray me place ?
Or—would you curse and spit into my face ?

September, 1939.

ENEMY CONSCRIPT

WHAT are we fighting for,
We fellows who go to war?
Fighting for Freedom's sake!
(You give me the belly-ache.)
Freedom to starve or slave!
Freedom! aye, in the grave.
Fighting for " hearth and home,"
Who haven't an inch of loam?
Hearth? Why even a byre
Can only be ours for hire.
Dying for future Peace?
Killing that killing cease?
To hell with such tripe, I say.
" Sufficient unto the day."

It ain't much fun being dead.
Better to lie in bed,
Cuddle up to the wife,
Making, not taking, life.

To the corpse that stinks in the clay,
Does it matter who wins the day ?
What odds if tyrants reign ?
They can't put irons on the brain.
One always can eat one's grub,
Smoke and drink in a pub.
There's happiness in a glass,
A pipe and the kiss of a lass.
It's the best we get anyhow,
In the life we are living now.

Who's wanting a hero's fate ?
To the dead cheers come too late.
Flesh is softer than steel ;
Wounds are weary to heal.
In the maniac hell of the fray
Who is there dares to say ?
" Hate will be vanquished by Love ;
God's in His Heaven above."

When those who govern us lead
The lads they command to bleed ;
When rulers march at the head,
And statesmen fall with the dead ;
When Kings leap into the fray,

Fight in the old-time way,
Perish beside their men,
Maybe, O maybe then
War will be part of the past,
Peace will triumph at last.

Meantime such lads as I,
Who wouldn't have harmed a fly,
Have got to get out and kill
Lads whom we bear no ill ;
As simple as we, no doubt,
Who seek what it's all about ;
Who die in defence of—what ?
Homes that they haven't got ;
Who perish when all they ask
Is to finish the daily task ;
Make bread for the little ones,
Not feed the greed of the guns,
When fields of battle are red,
And diplomats die in bed.

DON'T CHEER

Don't cheer, damn you! Don't cheer!
Silence! Your bitterest tear
Is fulsomely sweet to-day. . . .
Down on your knees and pray.

See, they sing as they go,
Marching row upon row.
Who will be spared to return,
Sombre and starkly stern ?
Chaps whom we knew —so strange,
Distant and dark with change ;
Silent as those they slew,
Something in them dead too.
Who will return this way,
To sing as they sing to-day.

Send to the glut of the guns
Bravest and best of your sons.
Hurl a million to slaughter,

Blood flowing like Thames water ;
Pile up pyramid high
Your dead to the anguished sky ;
A monument down all time
Of hate and horror and crime.
Weep, rage, pity, curse, fear—
Anything, but . . . don't cheer.

Sow to the ploughing guns
Seed of your splendid sons.
Let your heroic slain
Richly manure the plain.
What will the harvest be ?
Unborn of Unborn will see. . . .

Dark is the sky and drear. . . .
For the pity of God don't cheer.
Dark and dread is their way,
Who sing as they march to-day. . . .
Humble your hearts and pray.

L'ENVOI

Once more my sheaf of songs I tie,
And bid them gleefully good-bye,
And feel it will not give me pain,
To never look on them again.
With metronomic measure I
Have beat them out beneath the sky.
And though my facile rhyme I curse,
Sometimes I think they might be worse ;
But anyway, as in the past,
I vow that they will be my last.

For I have come to sixty-five,
Content to feel so much alive ;
And though grey-haired, I grieve to state
An unrepentent reprobate ;
Admiring lads who wench and wine,
But forced, alas! to toe the line ;
For I have learnt a thing or two,
As we old coves are bound to do.

I've come to know that storing health
Is better far than storing wealth ;
That smug success has little worth
Beside the simple joys of earth ;
That Fame is but a bubble brief,
And glory vain beyond belief ;
That it is good to eat and drink ;
That it is bad to over-think ;
That only stupid people claim
To take themselves with serious aim ;
That laughter is the God's best gift—
So to the Gods our laughter lift ;
Aye, though their wrath the Heaven's split,
They grant us Scorn, to laugh at it.

And so, frail creatures of a day,
Let's have a good time while we may,
And do the very best we can
To give one to our fellow man ;
Knowing that all will end with Death,
Let's joy with every moment's breath ;
And lift our heads like blossoms blythe
To meet at last the Swinging Scythe.

FINIS